T0380678

GREG MATTHEWS

WESTBOW
PRESS®
A DIVISION OF THOMAS NELSON
& ZONDERVAN

WestBow Press books may be ordered through booksellers or by contacting:

WestBow Press
A Division of Thomas Nelson & Zondervan
1663 Liberty Drive
Bloomington, IN 47403
www.westbowpress.com
1 (866) 928-1240

Christian Standard Bible

ISBN: 978-1-9736-8809-9 (sc)
ISBN: 978-1-9736-8810-5 (e)

Print information available on the last page.

WestBow Press rev. date: 04/13/2020

Introduction

Happy 70th Birthday
December 14, 2019

Dear Greg,

Since Easter Sunday - April 19, 1981- you have been writing devotionals. It was a huge influence on me as I watched you read the Word and then write your devotionals in the mornings. As I witnessed this transformation, the joy I saw in you helped me to look at myself and see the need for change in my life. Praise the Lord for His goodness to us! Somewhere up in the attic is a box with these early writings. But thanks to modern texting, the phone gave you a new tool. This devotional work is a collection of many of the devotionals you sent to our family in recent years. It's not in the exact order - changes had to be made for space and sometimes for an event. But these are your thoughts and I have loved reading them. They are special gifts to this family and future little Matthews grandchildren. They show us your heart, your love, and your devotion to the Lord and to us.

I love you!
Gwen

1 Samuel 10:6

"Then the Spirit of the LORD will come upon you, and you will prophesy with them and be turned into another man."

On this first day of a new year, this verse calls out to me. Here we see the calling of Saul as Israel's first king. But before he takes on that awesome position, God will do a work in him. Saul will in essence become a new man.

It puts me in mind of the verse Paul wrote in 2 Corinthians 5:17, "Therefore, if anyone is in Christ, he is a new creation; old things have passed away; behold, all things have become new."

When God calls us to Himself, He does a complete makeover, a total restoration. He equips us for new tasks with a new attitude. He sets our course in a new direction with new purpose and goals. He gives us abilities and gifts we never had before, while re-purposing the ones already present.

At the outset of this New Year, why not rejoice in this new life He has given and wait expectantly on the new thing He intends to do in each one of us in the coming 12 months.

Genesis 1

The first verses of Gods Holy Word give us important theology on which to anchor faith. God is preexistent. "In the beginning, God." He is already on the scene at the beginning. Thus, God is eternal. Never beginning. Never ending.

He is also present in the universe He created. "God created the ...". He is first source. First cause. From God all things come. Further, God is Spirit. We are told He hovered over the creation. He was present. He was actively engaged. It was His handiwork. The deist view of God is that He set systems in motion then checked out and let them function. Not according to this account.

Finally, God's creative method was to speak things, systems, objects, designs into being. "Then

God said ...". Everything in those six creative days He spoke into existence. Except the final piece: Man He formed from the dust of the ground. The uniqueness of how God created a unique being made by His Hands in the likeness of Himself.

This is basic theology that anchors a belief system to the truth about God. It is the foundational building block on everything to follow. As we journey through the Bible yet another time this year, let's always remember this first chapter of Genesis that puts the rest of the Scripture into its proper theological context. "In the beginning God".

Jeremiah 11:20

But, LORD of Armies, who judges righteously, who tests heart and mind...

This verse struck me this morning, the judgment of God. In addition to being a Creator, a Redeemer, a Provider, a Father, He is also a Judge. And scripture insists that God's judgments are wholly just. We are warned about judging others, for by the measure we judge, God will suspend His just judgments and use our judgment. I don't want to be judged by my own imperfect judgment. But His judgment is perfect and this verse gives us three reasons it is. He judges by a perfect measure (Himself). He not only weighs our actions, but he takes into account our reasons for doing them (testing the mind) and our emotive state (the heart).

All of it weighs into the scale of God's righteous judgment. So I can say with Abraham as he considered the judgment of Sodom and Gomorrah, "Shall not the judge of all the earth do right?" – Genesis 18:25

We live in a day when the cultural answer to that rhetorical question is a resounding "No!" Our culture puts God on trial as an unjust judge. It is vital that as Christians we trust in God as Judge, and be thankful that in Christ we will never fall under the weight of His eternal judgment. For we are forgiven by the blood of His Son.

1 Samuel 3:7

*Now Samuel did not yet know the LORD, because the word of
the LORD had not yet been revealed to him.*

This verse had a familiar ring this morning, knowing God when He reveals Himself through the Word. I was 31 years old and wrestling with my life when God revealed Himself through the Word to me. I was raised in church but had fallen away from Christ so that by the time I finished college there was no evidence of faith in my life. On this particular night, I was lying on my bed wrestling with a whole number of choices I had made in my career, as a husband and father and as a decent human being. I was failing at all four of them.

As I laid there a verse came across my mind, one I learned in Sunday school as a child. "Trust in the Lord with all your heart." (Proverbs 3:5) It was a message from Him. It gave me a new direction to pursue. It offered hope. I went to bed that night an agnostic and woke up in the morning a believer seeking a relationship with the Lord.

What I have always appreciated was the care given me as a child to plant God's Word in my life. This is so crucial for our children. For in due course, God can use the implanted Word to reveal Himself, just as He did for Samuel and for me

Exodus 12:13

*"The blood on the houses where you are staying will be a distinguishing
mark for you; when I see the blood, I will pass over you."*

The nation of Israel was preparing to leave centuries of slavery in Egypt. But first God would perform a final miracle to convince Pharaoh to release them; the destruction of the Egyptian first born. The blood on Israelite homes would protect their families from the death angel.

It is a picture of how God will in time redeem a future people from their bondage through the perfect sacrifice of His Son. And it is a promise that to be covered by the blood of Christ shed on the cross frees me from sin and its consequence, death. Without the sacrifice of Jesus on the cross I would remain under God's wrath. And in my case, it would be a multiplied wrath having understood God's great sacrifice without responding to it. I shudder to imagine the offense to God's grace. But thanks be to God: He has provided the covering of His only begotten Son's blood that enables us to come into His presence, forgiven and cleansed of all iniquity.

Is it any wonder that the color red is such a prominent feature of Christmas colors. Every time I see that color this Christmas season, I want to be reminded that Jesus' blood covers me.

2 Corinthians 4:16-18

16 Therefore we do not give up. Even though our outer person is being
destroyed, our inner person is being renewed day by day.
17 For our momentary light affliction is producing for us an
absolutely incomparable eternal weight of glory.
18 So we do not focus on what is seen, but on what is unseen. For
what is seen is temporary, but what is unseen is eternal.

This is the passage I read over and over to my mother as she battled dementia in her final two years. It always brought her comfort and even praise to the Savior. She recognized that even as her physical and mental abilities were deteriorating, there was an inner life being renewed and prepared for eternity. And she took great comfort in this. It brought her hope in an otherwise hopeless circumstance.

How can a person who is literally losing their hold on reality be comforted and even encouraged? By the Spirit through the Word. That is what the believer holds as hope, and the unbeliever as the stench of death. My mother's response to her dementia illustrates for me what this passage talks about. It is one of the miracles of God's salvation for the redeemed, the miraculous reversal of circumstances that faith in God alone can effect.

Mark 2:3-5

3 They came to him bringing a paralytic, carried by four of them.
4 Since they were not able to bring him to Jesus because of the crowd, they removed the roof above
him, and after digging through it, they lowered the mat on which the paralytic was lying.
5 Seeing their faith, Jesus told the paralytic, "Son, your sins are forgiven."

An interesting encounter Jesus had with four friends of a man who could not walk. How he came to be paralyzed Mark does not tell us. However it happened, this unfortunate man had the good fortune of having four friends who cared. Men of faith. Since this incident took place at the start of Jesus' public ministry, these four friends were alert to what was going on and had obviously heard about this miracle worker living amongst them. When Jesus came to their community, they acted. Jesus commends their "faith" in this passage. Two things to notice about this commendable faith. It acts. Faith is not passive. It moves people to take action.

Faith is also a witness. Jesus saw it. It was observable to others. So much more could be said about this elusive concept, faith. But these two things are good to start with. Faith acts. Faith is a witness to others. "O God, may my faith in You acquire these characteristics in the coming days, first to my family and then to my world."

Isaiah 61: 1-11

1 The Spirit of the Lord GOD is on me, because the LORD has anointed me
to bring good news to the poor. He has sent me to heal the brokenhearted,
to proclaim liberty to the captives and freedom to the prisoners;
2 to proclaim the year of the LORD's favor, and the day of our
God's vengeance; to comfort all who mourn,
3 to provide for those who mourn in Zion; to give them a crown of beauty instead of
ashes, festive oil instead of mourning, and splendid clothes instead of despair. And
they will be called righteous trees, planted by the LORD to glorify him.

4 They will rebuild the ancient ruins; they will restore the former devastations;
they will renew the ruined cities, the devastations of many generations.
5 Strangers will stand and feed your flocks, and foreigners will be your plowmen and vine dressers.
6 But you will be called the LORD's priests; they will speak of you as ministers of our
God; you will eat the wealth of the nations, and you will boast in their riches.
7 In place of your shame, you will have a double portion; in place of disgrace, they will rejoice
over their share. So they will possess double in their land, and eternal joy will be theirs..
8 For I the LORD love justice; I hate robbery and injustice; I will faithfully
reward my people and make a permanent covenant with them.
9 Their descendants will be known among the nations, and their posterity among the
peoples. All who see them will recognize that they are a people the LORD has blessed.
10 I rejoice greatly in the LORD, I exult in my God; for he has clothed me
with the garments of salvation and wrapped me in a robe of righteousness, as a
groom wears a turban and as a bride adorns herself with her jewels.
11 For as the earth produces its growth, and as a garden enables what is sown to spring up,
so the Lord GOD will cause righteousness and praise to spring up before all the nations.

In all the chaos and tumult of our present age, it is hopeful and encouraging to step into the prophet Isaiah's vision of what God has planned for this world. These prophecies from the 61st chapter of Isaiah will be fulfilled when Jesus returns.

So I say, "Maranatha. Come Lord Jesus!"

2 Corinthians 2:14-16

14 But thanks be to God, who always leads us in Christ's triumphal procession
and through us spreads the aroma of the knowledge of him in every place.
15 For to God we are the fragrance of Christ among those who are
being saved and among those who are perishing.
16 To some we are an aroma of death leading to death, but to others, an aroma of life leading to life.

Mixed messaging! It is a frustration. Often it is a tactic of manipulation. Sometimes rank injustice. We want straight talk. But interpreting a message can also lead to mixed understanding. That is what Paul says about a Christian life witness. Our lives should be a type of mixed message - one for the believer that reinforces salvation and eternal hope; another for the world that communicates God's judgment and a certain, eternal consequence for sin and unbelief.

It shouldn't be surprising that the Christian faith is under pressure and being attacked, not just here in our culture but around the world. We are literally the stench of death to unbelievers. That is why it is incumbent on us to make the hope of salvation clear to those who don't have faith in Christ, both in word and deed. That stench becomes sweet perfume as faith is added and forgiveness and eternal life are the result.

Zechariah 3:1

"Then he showed me the high priest Joshua standing before the angel of the LORD, with Satan standing at his right side to accuse him."

Satan has an insidious way of keeping people bound to evil.

He tempts us to sin, knowing our natural bent toward unrighteousness. When we respond, he then accuses us of having broken God's law and stand condemned for doing it. Temptation, accusation. What a terrible strategy to keep a person bound to evil.

This cycle repeats itself time and again, leaving a person resigned to its inevitability. "This is just who I am." It is one reason we see wrong behavior transformed into statements of identity. The gay person claims his behavior is his nature. The thief justifies himself by identifying as a bad boy. Behavior is explained as identity. A complete win for Satan. God enters this vicious cycle with mercy and grace. He offers to forgive the repentant sinner. But he offers even more. Look at verses 3-4.

3 Now Joshua was dressed with filthy clothes as he stood before the angel.
4 So the angel of the LORD spoke to those standing before him, "Take off his filthy clothes!" Then he said to him, "See, I have removed your iniquity from you, and I will clothe you with festive robes."

When God saves a person from their sins, He does more than forgive their guilt. He also gives a new identity represented here by the removal of their old, filthy clothing being replaced by clean, festive garments. This is a complete, divine transformation. And it breaks the cycle that Satan has used that binds us to evil. Because of His mercy and grace, we live in newness of life. Born again and clothed in His (Jesus') righteousness with a completely new identity.

Celebrate God's great salvation for a moment. And thank Him for a new identity in Christ.

Tahlon's cross, 2018

Proverbs 10:12

I try to read five chapters of the Bible a day. That enables me to read through it in a year. Today I read probably 150 Proverbs from Solomon's wise teachings in chapters 6-10. One jumped off the page in the 10th chapter.

12 Hatred stirs up conflicts, but love covers all offenses.

Doesn't God model this? He covers our offenses through Christ's redemptive work and His divine forgiveness. The alternatives would be frightful. Imagine God sitting around the heavenly host gossiping to the angels about my shortcomings and sinful behavior. Or if he used my transgressions against me by exposing them for all to see.

Worse still, where would I be if God left all my iniquity next to my name in what scripture calls "The Books" rather than writing my name in the Book of Life by forgiving and forgetting my sins.

Gossiping, holding onto offenses is too often the way we deal with offenses committed against us. God is not like that. Better to take the divine approach and forgive, release the offense, then forget about it.

Malachi 2:5

"My covenant with him was one of life and peace. And I gave these to him; it called for reverence, and he revered me and stood in awe of my name."

Here is a simple, spiritual equation that the prophet brings to us. It is one we ought to pay close attention to. God, on His side, offers us life and peace. That is abundant life and peace that passes understanding. He expects from us the other side of the equation .. reverence and awe. Fostering the knowledge of His greatness and His goodness.

Be constantly aware that our abundant life and matchless peace are His gifts and not our cleverness or superior techniques of living. So in the end, I become a deeply thankful person.

"Rejoice always, pray constantly, give thanks in everything; for this is God's will for you in Christ Jesus."
1 Thessalonians 5:16-18

Joshua 24:14-15

14 *"Therefore, fear the LORD and worship him in sincerity and truth. Get rid of the gods your fathers worshiped beyond the Euphrates River and in Egypt, and worship the LORD.*
15 *"But if it doesn't please you to worship the LORD, choose for yourselves today: Which will you worship — the gods your fathers worshiped beyond the Euphrates River or the gods of the Amorites in whose land you are living? As for me and my family, we will worship the LORD."*

Thoughts on this worship passage. The first, how we ought to approach God in worship. Sincerely. Also, our worship needs to be truthful or by encountering Him through His Word which is truth.

The last thought jumped off the page to me. It is a much quoted verse and captures the commitment to worship. "As for me and my family, we will worship the Lord." (v. 15). We will worship. That is volitional worship.

Remaining a worshipful Christian in our day needs these attitudes of worship: Sincerity, truth and volition ("we will").

Matthew 17:5-6

5 While he was still speaking, suddenly a bright cloud covered them, and a voice from the cloud said: This is my beloved Son, with whom I am well pleased. Listen to him!"
6 When the disciples heard this, they fell facedown and were terrified".

Consider the disciples response to the voice of God in that cloud. Terror. Abject fright. Not dissimilar from how the Israelite nation responded to the voice and presence of Yahweh at Mt Sinai when He have the 10 commandments.

They said to Moses, "You go up there. We want no part of this. Too frightening."

That made me consider how I approach God. It is not with dread or terror. An intermediary has removed the terror and replaced it with relational warmth, interest and even hopefulness. The danger now is being casual, even sacrilegious toward The Almighty.

And then I thought about the ways I can approach God. Obviously through Christ, our mediator. But also through the Word, another gracious avenue into His presence that removes the terror. Can you think of other ways we have access? And my attitude of approaching Him is also important. Hopeful. Worshipful. Submissive. Even boldly (Hebrews 4:16). Because of Christ, I need not come cowering in fear.

Isaiah 30:1

"Woe to the rebellious children! This is the LORD's declaration. They carry out a plan, but not mine; they make an alliance, but against my will, piling sin on top of sin."

Here is a dangerous spiritual condition… piling one sin on top of another. Getting under the pile of sin separates me progressively from a close walk with God. It creates the cycle of sin that results in sinning with impunity, a grievous spiritual condition.

God's antidote to sin is confession and faith in Christ's blood shed for sin on the cross. It is practicing 1 John 1:9 regularly. *"If we confess our sins, He is faithful and just to forgive us our sins and to cleanse us from all unrighteousness."* Being brought regularly to what Jesus did for me on the cross is a vital part of living the Christian life.

That was one thing I appreciated about our practice of celebrating the Lord's Supper every week at Spring Mountain Bible Church. A regular encounter with the emblems of my redemption, the bread and the wine, helped me root out sin in my life so that the condition of "sin upon sin" could not easily take hold.

Take a moment right now to confess any sin to Jesus that He wants to forgive and cleanse.

Psalm 51:12

"Restore the joy of your salvation to me and sustain me by giving me a willing spirit."

Here is a little teaching on the perseverance of the saints. As one of the pillars of Calvinism, the believer will in the end finish the course of faith and find eternal rest in the arms of Christ. Along the way, many pitfalls and temptations will be faced, but also overcome through God's grace and power. In this little verse, we find two key elements of the Spirit's work on our behalf to bring this blessed life result.

The first is emotional and deals with joy, specifically the joy of having sins forgiven, being given a new nature (of Christ) and the assurance of God's completed work of redemption in our lives. That is salvation. Saved from my past offenses, from the present temptations of this evil age and saved to an eternal future with Christ and the saints in glory. The knowledge and joy of this is a foundation for desiring and seeking it more.

Perseverance. A second work of the Holy Spirit is transformational in my weak and fallen spirit. As an abiding Presence in my life, the Holy Spirit quickens my will to desire and seek the salvation God has given me.

He is a partner in the redemptive work of salvation, the "senior partner". Such a necessary work too, for I find myself easily distracted and enticed into the worldly sins from which Christ saved me and ransomed me by Hisblood. But His blessed Spirit has been given to me as a guide and surety that though the way to eternal life may take some detours because of my wrong choices, it will end in the glorious presence of God.

Joy and a willing spirit. The Great work of God's Spirit in the life of every believer.

Brothers Joy, Ben and Asa

Matthew 13:14-17

14 *"Isaiah's prophecy is fulfilled in them, which says: You will listen and listen,*
but never understand; you will look and look, but never perceive.
15 *"For this people's heart has grown callous; their ears are hard of hearing, and they*
have shut their eyes; otherwise they might see with their eyes, and hear with their ears,
and understand with their hearts, and turn back — and I would heal them.
16 *"Blessed are your eyes because they do see, and your ears because they do hear.*
17 *"For truly I tell you, many prophets and righteous people longed to see the things*
you see but didn't see them, to hear the things you hear but didn't hear them."

One of the great privileges of being a born again child of God is understanding biblical truth. God's Word communicates to His people what we need for life and godliness. His Spirit instructs in our inner beings what He wants us to know and obey. It is good to take an inventory on how His Word impacts our lives. Having ears and eyes to see and hear revealed biblical truth is a powerful evidence of who we are: God's children taught by Him.

Matthew 18:3-6

3 *"Truly I tell you," he said, "unless you turn and become like*
children, you will never enter the kingdom of heaven.
4 *"Therefore, whoever humbles himself like this child — this one is the greatest in the kingdom of heaven.*
5 *"And whoever welcomes one child like this in my name welcomes me.*
6 *"But whoever causes one of these little ones who believe in me to fall away — it would be better for*
him if a heavy millstone were hung around his neck and he were drowned in the depths of the sea."

This biblical thought deals with things of utmost importance, my grandchildren. Jesus uses children to make key spiritual truths that resound in me.

The first truth: access to God must be through the unpretentiousness of the child. Humility.

Arrogance is something we grow into. Children don't seem to suffer that. And God values that in children and in us.

The second: dependence. Children come to us to have their needs met. And when we meet them, when we welcome their requests it is a godly response. Because that is the way God responds to us. He doesn't begrudge us. He just provides.

Thirdly: childlike vulnerability. They need our protection; physically, emotionally and spiritually. This teaching warns about failing in our protective responsibility in each of these three areas, a VERY serious deficiency.

I love my grandchildren. They are my absolute delight. I want to be part of their provision and protection. I also want to learn from the grace God has poured into them.

"Thank you, Father, for these gifts of life."

Happy Birthday Jesus, 2019

Job 38:8-11

8 Who enclosed the sea behind doors when it burst from the womb,
9 when I made the clouds its garment and total darkness its blanket,
10 when I determined its boundaries and put its bars and doors in place,
11 when I declared: "You may come this far, but no farther; your proud waves stop here"

The recent government report on the progress and effect of global warming had a lot to say about low lying coastal areas. It claims that if warming is permitted to continue, millions of Americans will be displaced by the rising waters on our coastlines. It declared that a man-made calamity is surely on the way if we don't act now.

I found this verse interesting this morning. God claims to have set those boundaries in place. Is it possible for man to undo the work of God? We will watch closely in the coming years the effects on our coastlines of climate change/global warming. I rather suspect authorities have overstated the danger and that the work of God in setting those boundaries will be affirmed.

Genesis 16:13

So she named the LORD who spoke to her:
"You are El-roi," for she said, "In this place,
have I actually seen the one who sees me?"

This little verse in the account of Hagar, the slave/concubine of Abraham has a deep spiritual truth. Hagar had run away from an abusive Sarah because the plan Sarah hatched to provide Abraham with an heir had caused problems. (Can anything good come from polygamy?)

As Hagar sat in the wilderness, God revealed Himself to her and gave her direction and hope. How many of us have had a similar encounter with God in difficult times? And that encounter has opened our eyes to "El Roi", the God who has always been watching over me and Who I can now apprehend. This is a conversion moment. Blind eyes seeing spiritual reality. Deaf ears hearing the Word of God. Stony hearts made flesh and inclined toward Him.

Take a moment to reflect on the El Roi moment of your life. Give God thanks for revealing Himself. And if there has never been that moment, ask Him to reveal Himself as El Roi, just as He did for Hagar so many years ago.

Psalm 71:6, 18

6 I have leaned on you from birth; you took me from my mother's womb. My praise is always about you.
18 Even while I am old and gray, God, do not abandon me, while I proclaim your
power to another generation, your strength to all who are to come.

Here in this wonderful Psalm we see the bookends of life (infancy/old age) given to God in praise. On this weekend of the March For Life, how crucial to affirm that God sees us as human beings from the womb. "Fetus" is a proper medical term that has taken on a political slant to deny the unborn their personhood. We call the unborn "babies" when extending rights to them. They are fetuses to those who would extinguish their rights. God sees us from womb to grave as human beings.

The second verse sets in place one of the key purposes of the aged - passing on the truths of God to generations that follow. My task is to be part of the spiritual formation of children (three sons) and grandchildren (five in all, soon a sixth) that God has blessed me with. That begins with defending their absolute, God-given right to life. Remove that most fundamental and precious right and everything that follows is lost completely. What a good time to step back and prayerfully thank our God for giving us the great gift of life. And to reaffirm an absolute commitment to defending it with all our heart, soul and mind.

Job 28:28

On Wednesdays my Bible reading takes me through the wisdom literature of Scripture: Job, Proverbs, Ecclesiastes, Songs, and finally Lamentations. As I read in the 28th chapter of Job today, there is a verse that briefly, succinctly and powerfully sums up nearly everything that is said about being wise in Scripture.

> *28 He said to mankind, "The fear of the LORD—that is wisdom.*
> *And to turn from evil is understanding."*

Fear God. Turn away from evil. Faith and action combined.
(Or as James would say faith and works).

List some ways you can repent of evil this day and ask Him for strength to obey:

1.

2.

3.

Acts 1:8

"But you will receive power when the Holy Spirit has come on you, and you will be my witnesses in Jerusalem, in all Judea and Samaria, and to the end of the earth."

Two certainties in this verse, guarantees from Jesus to His people. They will be witnesses of His grace and power. And to carry out that calling, they will be empowered by the Holy Spirit.

Spiritual Power in the Christian life is tied to our witness. We do so with words and deeds. The deeds of this spiritual power are character qualities: love, joy, peace, patience, goodness, kindness, gentleness, faithfulness, self control. (Galatians 5:22-23) These qualities manifest themselves in simple acts of kindness.

Then there are the words of witness, the message we bring to the world around us. That message focuses on the truth about God and what He is like as revealed by Scripture. "For God so loved the world that He gave His only begotten Son, that whoever believes in Him should not perish but have everlasting life." (John 3:16)

Jesus never called his followers to something He didn't also equip them to do. The question for me is, will I respond to His calling? Will I be His witness in word and deed?

Jeremiah 4:22

"For my people are fools; they do not know me. They are foolish children, without understanding. They are skilled in doing what is evil, but they do not know how to do what is good."

Much of Jeremiah's message to Israel is summarized by these words of extreme rebuke. Following a great repentance under King Josiah, the nation had again fallen into idolatry that would result in a 70 year exile in far off Babylon. So it isn't surprising the prophet says some mighty harsh things. But what nuggets to glean among the harsh condemnation. And here is one of them: "Children do not know to do what is good." That is the job of an effective parent, to teach their child how to do what is right and proper. It is easy to fall into the "don't" of parenting. Children seem to gravitate toward what they shouldn't do. And they need our correction. But we can't forget about teaching the "do's" of life.

One of Gwen's students gave her a gift this week. It was a package with a monogrammed plate, a bag of delicious cookies, a box of chocolates and a picture of that student and their family. The message said, "May the celebration of Christ's birth be a joyful reminder of God's great love." It was obviously a family project, probably the mom working with her two daughters to honor the people making positive inputs into her children's lives. A small but effective example of teaching kids how to do what is good.

Leviticus 11:44

"For I am the LORD your God, so you must consecrate yourselves and be holy because I am holy."

In our secular, pragmatic age it is easy to lose sight of this command God gives to His people Israel. Being holy means to be different in attitude, thought and action.

The difference is a reflection of the One in whom I have put my trust. It is branding that separates me from the culture around me.

My brand is "Christian". That designates a lifestyle that is Christ-like. My goal is to reveal Christ to those around me. In that sense I see holiness as a pursuit rather than an end.

Some days are better than others in this pursuit of being Christ-like.

But the effort remains. It is what we call perseverance.. a necessary component of holiness. Press on in holiness.

Make it be my primary pursuit this week.

1 Samuel 26:23

"The LORD will repay every man for his righteousness and his loyalty."

Consider these two virtues in the Christian life: righteousness and loyalty. The first, righteousness, is living by a code set by God Himself. It is embodying the virtues of the Ten Commandments, loving

God and loving others, and doing so on the basis of faith. Loyalty, the second virtue, is measured by our commitment to relationships, with God and each other. Righteousness enhances loyalty. It puts us in good favor with God. If righteousness is a plumb line, loyalty is the builder's level that keeps us straight with each other.

As I do construction projects, I often remember that Jesus' earthly occupation was a carpenter. He was adept at building things, measuring, leveling, attaching, fitting.

The plumb line in His life with The Father (righteousness) was perfectly true. So were the levels (loyalty) in all of His human relationships. I want to be more like Jesus. How about you?

"Lord Jesus, You set for us the perfect example to follow.

Grant us lessons as Your apprentices to build righteous and loyal lives that bring You honor and glory."

Judges 8:21

Zebah and Zalmunna said, "Get up and strike us down yourself, for a man is judged by his strength."

I was thinking about this proverbial statement this morning; being judged by strengths. There are different types of strength, the most obvious being physical strength. But there are others, as well. Strength of character. Moral strength. Strength of faith and conviction. How will others judge me? How will they evaluate my character, faith, my convictions. Do I possess these things weakly? Or is there a tenacity that is obvious? A man is judged by his strengths.

But we are also observed in our weaknesses. People should be less inclined to judge the weakness since we all suffer them. But there is a human tendency to gossip about and put down other people's weakness. Harsh judgment.

Birthday honors is the means we have in our family of reinforcing our individual strengths. It is an effort to define each other by the ongoing grace God gives us. May we continue to judge by our strengths and forgive our limitations and weakness.

Psalm 9:1

I will thank the LORD with all my heart;
I will declare all your wondrous works.

I like this line of the 9th hymn. It links the heart and the tongue. It brings worship together with witness. I am reminded about an incident I heard at the party for two of my grandsons.

I asked my son about a family who attended the party.

He told me they were neighbors they had met and started up a friendship. A discussion about God had ensued and they came to church. The hope is they might one day attend their home group and grow in God's grace and knowledge. And if they don't know Jesus as Savior, that there will be that defining moment, too.

Worship yielding witness. A thankful heart that yields a grateful, expressive tongue.

"Pray also for me, that the message may be given to me when I open my
mouth to make known with boldness the mystery of the gospel."
Ephesians 6:19

Psalm 6:1

"LORD, do not rebuke me in your anger; do not discipline me in your wrath."

When I remember disciplining my children in anger I cringe. Spanking needs to be meted out with careful consideration. The emotion of anger violates that responsibility.

In time, I learned to send the boys to their room before disciplining them. It gave me time to consider the offense, my reaction to the situation and the best course of action to get a behavior change or lesson into their lives.

2 Be gracious to me, LORD, for I am weak; heal me, LORD, for my bones are shaking;

Sometimes a prayer gave the Lord time to influence my reaction and change the course of the punishment I was planning. Mercy can, at times, triumph.

And we tried to conclude punishment episodes with prayer for God's wisdom and counsel to bring life change into the correction. Parenting is an awesome responsibility and a difficult task. I'm praying for all of you parents as you seek to raise these precious children.

Job 38:36

"Who put wisdom in the heart or gave the mind understanding?"

This is God's rhetorical answer to Job's accusations about divine injustice. Bad things do happen to good people. But that is not a reason to accuse God. I was thinking about the role of education in our children's lives. Think about how much effort will be put into educating our grandchildren over the next two decades!

We will drive thousands of miles and spend thousands of dollars to insure they have a suitable understanding of scholastic truths. But at the heart of wisdom, as this verse clearly states, is the Person of God. Solomon put it similarly, *"The fear of the Lord is the beginning of wisdom". (**Proverbs 9:10**)*

Let's remember the theological heart of true education.

Teach the children to know and fear the Lord. And remember to add prayer to the miles and dollars that will be spent in the coming years. Spending time on our knees will yield the greatest results in these children's minds and hearts.

Isaiah 55:3

Who doesn't love the book of Isaiah .. *"For unto us a child is born .."(Isaiah 9:6); "All we like sheep have gone astray." (Isaiah 53:6).* So many wonderful verses we hang our faith on. Here is another from the 55th chapter.

"Pay attention and come to me; listen, so that you will live. I will make a permanent covenant with you on the basis of the faithful kindnesses of David."

Four things this verse reveals about God that should make us love Him more.

1. He is approachable. God invites us into personal and eternal relationship with Him. Jesus said in Matthew 11:28 - *"Come to me, all who are weary and burdened and I will give you rest."* God's eternal arms are always open to us so we might run to Him.

2. He is the source of life; "so that you will live." Living apart from God is the greatest error a person could make.

He is the "author of life". And in Him, *"we live and move and have our being."* Acts 17:28. Rejection of Him is literally suicide; spiritually, emotionally, relationally and ultimately physically.

3. The basis of every relationship with God is His promises and covenants. "I will make a permanent covenant". What an amazing divinity. God could be capricious with us (as the Greeks thought their gods to be). But He is perfectly consistent with His promises and expectations. And look, the covenant is everlasting.

4. And finally God is kind. In fact, kindness on kindness. The verse refers to His faithful kindness. He doesn't change His attitude toward us from day to day. Faithfulness is the foundation of God's love, kindness, grace, mercy.

Never changing. What a wonderful God we see in this verse! Easy to worship such a Divine Being. An additional thought from Isaiah 66 this morning.

2 "My hand made all these things, and so they all came into being. This is the LORD's declaration. I will look favorably on this kind of person: one who is humble, submissive in spirit, and trembles at my word."

Three things that God finds pleasing in a believer. Humility, submissiveness and respect for His Word.

Mark 8: 18-21

18 "Do you have eyes and not see; do you have ears and not hear? And do you not remember?
19 "When I broke the five loaves for the five thousand, how many baskets
full of leftovers did you collect?" "Twelve," they told him.
20 "When I broke the seven loaves for the four thousand, how many
baskets full of pieces did you collect?" "Seven," they said.
21 And he said to them, "Don't you understand yet?"

The disciples were slow to learn the lessons their rabbi tried to teach them. Here is a case in point. A great task was accomplished - feeding the multitudes with scant resources. Jesus performed the miracle twice for them in a relatively short period of time. But they apparently did not understand the significance or meaning of these miracles. "Don't you understand yet?"

Let's give it a stab. In the hands of Jesus a little is always enough. Scarcity gives way to abundance when the resource is given to Him. Am I ever tempted to think, "The problem is too great. The solutions too few." That thinking yields a type of hopeless paralysis. Jesus offers his disciples a theocentric world view that places divine power and will at the center. And it offers us options of faith if we will believe. Jesus says, *"All things are possible to him who believes"* (Mark 9:23). Good to test that faith through prayer for the impossible.

2 Corinthians 13:5

Test yourselves to see if you are in the faith. Examine yourselves. Or do you yourselves not recognize that Jesus Christ is in you? — unless you fail the test.

The Apostle Paul brings a challenging word this morning. Self examination. Scripture cautions us about examining and judging each other. Instead, it calls on each believer to test their own faith .. to identify the life of Christ in my own life.

Here is the need for being in God's Word consistently. The Bible is a Christian's guide for godly, Christ-like living. It is our primer. It is the mirror by which we can see His image being established in who we are. I'm so thankful God gives me do-overs. As often as I fail the self- examination God will forgive and offer me another course on His righteousness; another opportunity to pass the test.

And one day to graduate to that life to come.

Genesis 31:2

And Jacob saw from Laban's face that his attitude toward him was not the same as before.

I love the family photos we had taken recently. Seeing our clan all gathered with smiling faces (that photographer knows how to photoshop the images, although she put my head on wrong!) really brings me joy.

Our faces are windows into our souls. They often tell the story to others of how we are doing on the inside, in the secret place. Nonverbal communication can be as powerful as the actual words that come out of my mouth. They visually illustrate what we say.

Being careful with both my words and my "looks" is a lesson I need to be reminded about. Having a loving look is a crucial part of maintaining our relationships.

Our Family, 2018

Isaiah 40:28-31

A favorite passage of mine from Isaiah 40 this morning.

28 Do you not know? Have you not heard?
The LORD is the everlasting God, the Creator
of the whole earth. He never becomes faint or weary;
there is no limit to his understanding.

29 He gives strength to the faint and strengthens the powerless.
30 Youths may become faint and weary, and young men stumble and fall,
31 but those who trust in the LORD
will renew their strength; they will soar on wings like eagles; they will
run and not become weary, they will walk and not faint.

Reverse the order of blessing God brings to us in the 31st verse and you have quite a progression. From walk to run to soaring to total renewal. Amazing what God's grace can do in the life of one who trusts in Him.

Will that be me this week? Or you?

Zephaniah 1:6

Zephaniah is a short little book that is easy to overlook (or even find) in the Old Testament prophets. But it is packed with nuggets.

6 "and those who turn back from following the LORD, who do not seek the LORD or inquire of him."

The context is God stretching out His hand against this sort of person rather using His hand to help them. It is a good warning to examine life and faith. God rewards those who press on, look up and maintain hope. May He find that in me .. and in all of you too.

1 Chronicles 3:10

10 Solomon's son was Rehoboam; his son was Abijah, his son Asa, his son Jehoshaphat,
11 his son Jehoram, his son Ahaziah, his son Joash ..

And on and on. Reading this morning in a section of the Bible that deals with genealogies. A little tedious but it reminds me to pray for the sons of my sons (and a daughter too):

- Bless Tahlon in his school work today, Lord. Help him grasp the truth he is receiving, especially Your Word being hidden in his heart.

- Protect Ben as he explores and examines his world. Give him new insights to understand Your marvelous creation and how You have positioned him in it.

- Show Declan the value of his new school and group experience. Help him adjust to a wider world than just the protective family he has experienced thus far.

- Bring to Asa's mind new words and concepts that will enable him to communicate with us and also with You. Fill his mouth with praise and thanksgiving.

- And protect Rilynn in these initial days of living, eating and breathing in the life You have graciously given to her.

- And for the little one still waiting to be born, protect him and bring him safely into our family in the days to come.

Enable all of these children to come to the point of trusting in You as their Savior and then following You daily as Lord. This I ask in Jesus name and for His sake ...

Happy 70th, Greg, 2019

Proverbs 18:13

"The one who gives an answer before he listens - this is foolishness and disgrace for him."

This is such sound wisdom for our relationships! Open my ears before engaging my tongue. Being quick to speak out is a warning scripture often gives. In James 1:19 we learn *"quick to listen, slow to speak, slow to anger."* Human indignation does not produce righteousness. My tendency is to construct an argument in my mind instead of carefully listening to the perspective of the other person. Better to get that other perspective before building a response.

Jeremiah 29:7

"Pursue the well-being of the city I have deported you to. Pray to the LORD on its behalf, for when it thrives, you will thrive."

This is a letter the prophet sent to the Israelites in exile in Babylon. It is wise counsel for all-time. As Christians our citizenship and allegiance should be first given to the kingdom of God.

But we are also citizens of societies in this world. And here is instruction to be good citizens that make the nation we are in prosperous, safe and in our case free. Free to worship. Free to speak and witness. Free to associate with whoever we desire.

Christians never tear down. We build up. We are not to be problems. Rather, we offer solutions. We pay taxes. We defend justice. We vote our biblical values. We should be the best of citizens even as our allegiance is elsewhere.

Psalm 22:1

1 My God, my God, why have you abandoned me?
Why are you so far from my deliverance and from my words of groaning?
2 My God, I cry by day, but you do not answer, by night, yet I have no rest.

***Psalm 23:1** The LORD is my shepherd; I have what I need.*
2 He lets me lie down in green pastures; he leads me beside quiet waters.
3 He renews my life; he leads me along the right paths for his name's sake.

Remarkable that these two songs are located back to back. The first is Jesus' cry on the cross as He bore the sins of the world as His Father turned away from His sin-bearing Son. Yet the very next song celebrates the nearness and protection of God. He is here for you!

Romans 4:25

"He was delivered up for our trespasses and raised for our justification."

Salvation in God's redemptive design accounts of necessity for two things: the sin and the sinner. Because of Who God is, both must be dealt with. God is holy. He cannot bear the presence of sin. He abhors sin. And wherever sin raises its ugly head, God will oppose it. It is the sole focus of the divine, moral crusade.

Not only is God holy, he is thrice holy. When the angels address him in Isaiah 6, they sing holy, holy, holy. It is the scriptural way of asserting totality. So when the Romans verse speaks of Jesus Christ being delivered up for our transgressions (sin), it is God's only means of waging war against human sin. Christ took upon Himself the sin of the world. *"You are to name him Jesus, because he will save his people from their sins."* Matthews 1:21. That is what took place on the cross when Jesus died. Sin was paid for in full. One death, His death, accounted for all of our sin.

But a second work was required to complete the work of salvation: that being the guilt of the sinner. We stood guilty for having transgressed Gods law. In today's verse in Romans, God justifies sinners through the resurrection of Jesus Christ.

How does that happen? How does Jesus coming back to life having suffered the penalty for my sin make me righteous (justified) before God. Because without that divine justification, I cannot enter His presence. I'm not sure how that happens or why. I only know the Scripture says it does happen. So by faith I believe and receive it.

Forgiven and justified. The complete work of salvation. So thankful to the Lord Jesus Christ who died and rose again to accomplish all that for us.

2 Thessalonians 2:16

A little benediction for this precious family.

> 16 "May our Lord Jesus Christ himself and God our Father, who has loved
> us and given us eternal encouragement and good hope by grace,
> 17 encourage your hearts and strengthen you in every good work and word."

Did you notice the prayer related to our hearts, our hands (work) and our mouths (words). May all three work together in service to Christ and be used to build each other up in the faith.

Mark 4:22

> "For there is nothing hidden that will not be revealed, and nothing
> concealed that will not be brought to light."

The political spectrum cynically talks about transparency using it as a club to bash the opponent. Neither side of our politics has any intention of opening up their machinations to public scrutiny.

But they are not alone! I keep most of my private sin in the closet. And so do you. Hiding wrongdoing is a form of self-protection, at least that's what it seems to be. Of course, I can't hide my wrongdoings from God. He knows. And He offers me an alternative to what this verse says will ultimately happen, being exposed for who I truly am.

Forgiveness. If I will confess my shameful ways, God will forgive and cleanse. In another passage we are told He *"will remember my sins no more."* Jeremiah; 31:34.

That's a deal I am desperate to take!

Matthew 5:5

"Blessed are the meek,
For they shall inherit the earth."

This is a completely counter intuitive statement. Of all the "blessed" statements in these Beatitudes, this one most challenges our reason. How can meek people ever gain supremacy? There must be an ownership transfer coming whereby this transaction could take place. Meek people in our world aren't exactly on the ascendency.

So Jesus is making a prophetic statement here. He seems to say that the powerful-corrupt that rule and possess in our age are a passing phenomena. And that a future age will install leaders and authority of an entirely different character. Meek, gentle leadership.

Wouldn't I love a president who did all the things President Trump does and yet was meek in character. Of course, in the rough and tumble age we live in, it probably can't or won't happen.

But for an age to come, it offers me hope.

"Your kingdom come. Your will be done."
Matthew 7:10

Psalm 61:5

"God, you have heard my vows; you have given a heritage to those who fear your name."

I have thought much in the last few days about the heritage of godliness in our family and where it came from. It doesn't appear to have been from either John B. or Lorenzo John Matthews whose gravestones I visited on Thursday. At least there is no mention of God/Christ or Bible verses on their tombstones. Neither of my grandfathers were Jesus followers when they were married, Matthews or Smart. But both came to faith shortly thereafter through the witness of my grandmothers. That thread of faith in our family ran through the women, Olive Matthews and Mary Alice Smart. Nearly every one of their children bore the evidence of faith in Christ. So grateful for that heritage: a godly grandmother and a mother who would raise her family in the fear of the Lord.

Great-great grandfather, Busti, New York

Luke 4-6

This morning in my reading in Luke's gospel account of Jesus, I found four Names for the Savior in three chapters. Here they are for your consideration and prayer (we are told to pray in His name so consider these).

4:34 *"I know who you are — the Holy One of God!"*

4:41 *Also, demons were coming out of many, shouting and saying, "You are the Son of God!"*

5:24 *"But so that you may know that the Son of Man has authority on earth to forgive sins ..."*

6:5 *Then he told them, "The Son of Man is Lord of the Sabbath."*

List the names and may you be blessed by that Name above every name.

1.

2.

3.

4.

Philippians 1:6

*"I am sure of this, that he who started a good work in you will carry
it on to completion until the day of Christ Jesus."*

If you are like me, there remains a constant battle in the Christian life to actually be what Scripture calls me to. This battle is waged on a variety of fronts .. my mind and imagination, the presence of temptations and a tempter, the old nature which the Bible calls the flesh that is in conflict with the Holy Spirit controlling the new nature.

This struggle is waged at the spiritual level, the emotional and sometimes even the physical. They all interact since together they comprise a human being. I celebrate small victories in this struggle with sin and lament setbacks and defeats. It is the dynamic of worship and repentance. I appreciate the way Christ Church in Greensboro has a time of public repentance in each worship service! Jesus prayer *"lead us not into temptation"* (Matthew 6:13) which can also be translated "let us not fall into temptation" offers a battle plan. I need that way forward at times. And this 6th verse is a hope, a blessed hope, that keeps me moving forward in this impossible Christian experience.

Paul tells us plainly that there will be ultimate victory .. that these light and momentary trials will end in absolute victory in the day of Christ Jesus. That is a day when He fully reigns in my life, in my world and the kingdom of heaven is realized in a renewed and redeemed world.

Jeremiah 33:2

2 *"The LORD who made the earth, the LORD who forms it to*
establish it, the LORD is his name, says this:
3 *"Call to me and I will answer you and tell you great and incomprehensible things you do not know.*

What a powerful truth that motivates me to pray. The God who made and maintains this world and everything in it invites me to call out to Him. In response, He will answer.

That alone is amazing .. why a great God would bother to listen to my prayer. But He does. He leans down and puts His ear to me. Then He acts on that prayer.

Make a prayer list today that you offer up to Him:

1.

2.

3.

4.

Psalm 66:9

"He keeps us alive and does not allow our feet to slip."

I thought about this verse this morning as we reflected on Brooke and her friend's amazing 26.2 mile marathon run yesterday. We met the runners at the 20 and 22 mile markers and they looked amazingly fit, smiling, hugging children. I was shocked expecting to see a near death experience.

After the race I asked Brooke how she felt at that point, that she looked so good. But her report:

she was suffering greatly, feeling like death warmed over. Still, she had pushed through the pain at mile 22 to reach her goal. "He keeps us alive .."

I also asked her if she ever stumbled on the course. That could have ended her run on this momentous day. How could a person go mile after mile on a bad ankle or knee? But injuries to her feet, ankles and knees had not happened. Her knees didn't even swell much after the 4 1/2 hour ordeal was completed.

"He does not allow our feet to slip." I know the verse uses the physical to illustrate the spiritual. And what an illustration our brave daughter-in-law gave us in Charleston yesterday.

Proverbs 22:6

"Start a youth out on his way; even when he grows old he will not depart from it."

Tuesdays are special, designated days to pray for my children and grandchildren. So receiving pictures this week from family members reminded me to pray and do so earnestly. This Proverb gives some wise direction to my prayers.

Each of these precious gifts has their own "way" as the scripture says. Finding that unique direction is a task for parents and grandparents. Then developing and training each of their peculiar gifts and attributes is the instruction of this wise counsel. One thing is certain about these Matthews children: They are each unique. And they are blessed with wonderful attributes. Their natural abilities must be bathed in prayer and training. Parents are the frontline trainers/teachers. I want to join you in bringing these precious ones to the throne of grace for the mercy and grace God alone can dispense in their lives.

That is a family team from the biblical perspective. Parents training, grandparents praying. Both modeling with their godly lives. And that is how I pray for my children and myself that we would be good and godly examples to the next Matthews generation so they can see and experience the Christian faith in their homes and family.

1 Thessalonians 1:3

"We recall, in the presence of our God and Father, your work produced by faith, your labor motivated by love, and your endurance inspired by hope in our Lord Jesus Christ."

In the famous 1 Corinthians 13 passage on love, Paul says the three building blocks of Christianity are faith, hope and love. This verse connects the three in an interesting and dynamic way. God gives me a vision or task in life as an expression of faith, referred to here as "work". It could be marriage, family, serving God, career. But it is a God-given calling, an exercise of faith. Giving myself wholeheartedly to that calling - laboring at it - is what Paul says is the expression of love. I didn't really begin to love my wife until I did so whole-heartedly expecting nothing in return. Labor motivated by love. In my case, I needed the love of God to flood my heart before it was able to begin to truly love her.

The third leg is hope, expressed here as endurance or the refusal to give up. Hope sets its gaze on the finish line and endures. Think of Brooke running that marathon in Charleston. She had to keep her focus on the finish to endure the pain of the run. Hope that empowers amazing feats. It is like that in our calling: husband, wife, parent, employee, church member. Having our eye on finishing well is the fuel of hope. Faith, love and hope - three key aspects of living well the Christian life.

Numbers 6:23-26

Here is my prayer for this precious family today... one of the great prayers of all Scripture from.

23 "Tell Aaron and his sons, 'This is how you are to bless the Israelites. You should say to them,
24 "May the LORD bless you and protect you;
25 "may the LORD make his face shine on you
and be gracious to you;
26 "may the LORD look with favor on you
and give you peace."

The book of Numbers is easily overlooked when reading through the Bible because of the lengthy chapters describing all the tribes and clans and temple procedures. They seem to lack relevance in our day. But to do so would be to miss prayers like this one. Puts me in mind of Paul's statement:

"All scripture is inspired by God and is profitable for teaching, for
rebuking, for correcting, for training in righteousness."
2 Timothy 3:16

2 Samuel 12:12

"You acted in secret, but I will do this before all Israel and in broad daylight.'"

This morning's scripture points toward an uncomfortable reality in most of our lives - secret sin. Of course, the very idea is an illusion because there is One who knows our every thought, let alone our actions. But we are easily deluded by the dark side of our natures. All sin breaks down fellowship with God and each other. Secret sin does that in an insidious way as it gives us the temporary impression that all is right. We compartmentalize iniquity. Hiding sin leads to an even worse result; ignoring sin altogether.

When Nathan the prophet addressed King David's sin with Bathsheba, he delivered the judgment no secret sinner wants to hear: "you will be exposed!" In another passage we are told, *"Be sure: your sins will find you out!"* Numbers 32:23. David's initial sin of adultery progressed into murder as he tried to hide it. Unconfessed sin has real power over our moral choices, leading along a path of increased wrongdoing. God's plan for secret sin is in 1 John 1:9. *"If we confess our sins, he is faithful and righteous to forgive us our sins and to cleanse us from all unrighteousness."* The worst place to hide sin is before God. He knows. Take a moment to put that wonderful verse into action. Confess and be cleansed. Then live righteously.

Jeremiah 6:16

Thus says the LORD: "Stand in the ways and see,
And ask for the old paths, where the good way is,
And walk in it; Then you will find rest for your souls.
But they said, 'We will not walk in it.'

Why am I a conservative? Why do I tend toward the ideas, values and norms of the past? And distrust the latest-greatest ideas?

This verse captures a rationale for traditional values. Over time, these ideas have stood the test. They have been tried, adapted, examined and proven useful. And true.

Theologically, doctrine about God and man is given in the Scriptures. While modern scholarship would reinterpret the Bible, and there is some value in re-examining texts in light of subsequent scholarship, the core of biblical truth remains unchanged. It places me squarely in the traditional-conservative camp theologically.

This is what the verse refers to as the old ways. Thinking about myself, my place in the world, relationships at home, in the church, in the culture. These are defined in God's Word. It places me at the traditional-conservative end of the spectrum.

Proverbs 25:15

"A ruler can be persuaded through patience, and a gentle tongue can break a bone."

Consider how these two character qualities, patience and soft speech, collaborate in conflict situations. Being patient is dialing back my timetable for seeing the other person change. It is trusting deeply the emerging truth of a matter and letting that define and judge the conflict.

We live in an age of immediacy and have built our lives in such a way. Instant results are expected. If the computer runs slowly, it sours me. (Remember the old 386 and 486 computers of 25 years ago!).

Microwaves buy us a little extra time in the kitchen. But relationships aren't wired like that. They require a time-tested process of mutual agreements where patience is a necessary component.

A gentle tongue is the level ground that patience can travel on. *"A gentle tongue turns away wrath."* Proverbs 15:1. Anger is a major pothole to smooth relationships. Gentle speech allows patience to bring about the peaceful resolution we want.

Numbers 11:23

The LORD answered Moses, "Is the LORD's arm weak? Now you will see whether or not what I have promised will happen to you."

In this passage, Moses faced yet another crisis (they seemed endless!) as the Israelites venture off to their promised land. The people now want to return to Egypt. The food was better there. On this journey there was only this manna to eat. And though it is nutritious, they were sick of it. Rebellion is in the air. What God had provided .. the heavenly food .. was not sufficient. "Give us meat!", they demand. And God told Moses He would do that. But how? Where in this desolate wilderness could meat be found for a couple million people?

Are we so different from the Israelites? Sometimes God's provisions don't satisfy our desires. We want more. And unfortunately it is sometimes those very desires we left behind when we followed Jesus. Yet in His grace He will supply our wants and needs in ways we can't possibly foresee. "Is the Lord's arm too weak?" Never. The better question is, "Do I believe He can supply my every need?"

Luke 22:32

"But I have prayed for you that your faith may not fail. And you, when you have turned back, strengthen your brothers."

How often in life do I find myself re-treading paths that I should not be on. I have repented before of a misdeed or a sin and here it is again, staring me in the face. This verse gives me renewed determination to press forward in the pursuit of holiness and press into the arms of the Lord Jesus. "I have prayed for you." What sweet, encouraging words from a Savior/High Priest who even now sits at the right hand of the throne of God .. and prays for me.

How would you want Jesus to pray for you today in your struggle against sin? Consider writing a brief prayer of confession, thanking Jesus that you are forgiven.

(Write prayer here)

Dear Jesus,

Romans 15:13

*"Now may the God of hope fill you with all joy and peace as you believe so
that you may overflow with hope by the power of the Holy Spirit."*

Living without hope is one of the greatest dangers and tragedies in life. Hope enables me to negotiate the trials and troubles I face. It ushers me into a better tomorrow when today has failed me. Hope is an anchor for my wayward soul. It grounds me to truth by letting me wander away only so far. And I like to wander .. wanderlust.

Hope is that reminder of what God has and will do in our lives. The most blessed hope is God's promise that death is not final .. that there is life beyond death. Without the hope of resurrection, we are to be greatly pitied as people engaged in pipe dreams. If there is no resurrection, the epicurean philosophy makes better sense - "eat, drink and be merry."

But hope guides me into the narrow path that leads to eternal life. Three great concepts endure in the biblical worldview. Faith, hope and love. The greatest is love as the Apostle reminds us. But hope can't be overlooked. It is a marker – a signpost - that keeps me pressing on toward the upward call of God in Christ Jesus.

2 Timothy 1:7

"For God has not given us a spirit of fear, but one of power, love, and sound judgment."

These are the qualities to expect when our lives are governed by the Holy Spirit. And what an attractive life He produces!

- A life of power that reveals inner strength. Being strong in convictions, in faith. Who doesn't want to be around that type of person?

- A life of love. It is the mark of a Christian led by the Holy Spirit producing the wonderful fruit of love …

In our family life.

In our church.

In our community.

- A life of sound judgment. With all the knowledge in our world, what seems to be lacking is wisdom. This is living by the Proverbs and bearing the lasting fruit of such a life.

2 Timothy 4:2

"Preach the word; be ready in season and out of season; rebuke, correct,
and encourage with great patience and teaching."

A brief word for parents. Be biblical in your child's training. Anchor the precepts you give the children to God's Word. It is your strongest authority when they ask the inevitable "but why?" And training children should be a balance of rebuke (when they are naughty), of correction (when they are in error) and encouragement (when they are on the right path).

Psalm 92:1

1 It is good to give thanks to the LORD, to sing praise to your name, Most High, 2
to declare your faithful love in the morning and your faithfulness at night,
3 with a ten-stringed harp and the music of a lyre.
4 For you have made me rejoice, LORD, by what you have done; I
will shout for joy because of the works of your hands.
5 How magnificent are your works, LORD, how profound your thoughts!

Some thoughts to guide worship on this Sunday morning.

Focus on God's works and His Word to offer Him the thanks and praise that belong to Him alone.

Number 32:23

"But if you don't do this, you will certainly sin against the LORD; be sure your sin will catch up with you."

The situation: Israel has defeated five kingdoms on the east side of the Jordan River. Two of the tribes asked for this land to be apportioned to them. Moses is making sure they aren't trying to avoid the battles to come for the land west of the Jordan. He makes them promise to engage fully with the Israelite armies to defeat all the kings in the remainder of the land. He delivers this powerful warning to them. A good warning to us as well. Sin catches up to us. We may think that evil can remain hidden in our closets. But it won't. God always sees. And eventually, the matter will come to light.

Yesterday I was sitting next to a young man on the flight to Boston. The subject of the Patriots came up. The owner of the Patriots was just arrested for soliciting prostitution, a big embarrassment to him and the fans. My seat partner was amazed how stupid such a successful man could be, but that he probably thought his wealth would keep the matter private. I quoted this verse in Numbers. We agreed it is true, at least in this case. It's true for all of us and a good lesson to teach our children when they sin and try to lie and conceal.

"Be sure your sin will catch up to you."

Song of Songs 2:15

"Catch the foxes for us —the little foxes that ruin the vineyards —for our vineyards are in bloom."

Writing devotional thoughts from this piece of biblical wisdom literature can be a challenge. The entire book is a love conversation between Solomon and one of his MANY wives/concubines. So for monogamists like me, it's hard to take seriously. But this idea jumped out this morning - "the little foxes that ruin the vineyard." The vineyard in this analogy is the relationship between a man and woman. And small things can enter that relationship to steal away the best fruit.

What are these little foxes? Perhaps lack of attention to the needs of the other person. A little oversight that removes good will. Perhaps the absence of gratitude for little favors done. Easy to overlook the small things (cleaning a mess, fixing a broken something) that takes the joy out of the task and turns it into just another duty. Little foxes.

"Lord, show us the small ways through inattention that we spoil our relationships so that they may continue to bear the fruit of love and grace."

Ezekiel 36:25-27

25 "I will also sprinkle clean water on you, and you will be clean. I will cleanse you from all your impurities and all your idols.
26 "I will give you a new heart and put a new spirit within you; I will remove your heart of stone and give you a heart of flesh.
27 "I will place my Spirit within you and cause you to follow my statutes and carefully observe my ordinances."

Like the nation of Israel, we live in a time of great iniquity. Evil seems to grow daily not just in our nation but also around the world. It seems to also take root in us who are called by His name - Christians. The danger is to lower our expectations of righteousness and godliness, becoming like those around us.

God has a different plan for His people. And it begins with spiritual renewal. He doesn't want us to live compromised lives. He doesn't want our values shaped by our culture. He wants to set our feet on the pathway to righteousness and holiness. These verses are a great encouragement that even in the depths of sin, God can renew our faith and set us on that upward calling we once received in Christ Jesus. Look at all the amazing things He will do for those who repent. Forgive, Cleanse. New heart. New spirit. Abiding Presence. God's work of forming a new person in Christ is truly a thing of beauty and wonder. Let Him do it in you and me today. Amen?

Titus 2:11-14

11 For the grace of God has appeared, bringing salvation for all people,
12 instructing us to deny godlessness and worldly lusts and to live in
a sensible, righteous, and godly way in the present age,
13 while we wait for the blessed hope, the appearing of the glory of our great God and Savior, Jesus Christ.
14 He gave himself for us to redeem us from all lawlessness and to cleanse for
himself a people for his own possession, eager to do good works.

One of the great passages that clearly explain the meaning of Christmas and Easter. It summarizes in very few words what it means to be a Christian. We read this today at EvenRidge with our dear grandson Tahlon, who is learning what it means to follow the Lord Jesus Christ. Gwen had the privilege of leading him to Christ at the Easter season two years ago. And we have witnessed his steady progress in the faith. What a joy!

EvenRidge Treehouse Project, 2018

Deuteronomy 2:7

"For the LORD your God has blessed you in all the work of your hands. He has
watched over your journey through this immense wilderness. The LORD your God
has been with you this past forty years, and you have lacked nothing."

Reading this verse tonight in northern Vermont brings a fresh sense of gratitude and confidence in the Lord. As we rested at EvenRidge this past weekend, Gwen and I marveled at all that God has done for us over the 46+ years of marriage. It is summarized in this short verse: *"What do you have that you did not receive?"* 1 Corinthians 4:7. Even the things we have earned through our work is a gift. Without our health and soundness of mind, that work could not have happened.

But our bounty goes far beyond our work. Our children and grandchildren are divine presents from a gracious God. Our retirement both from teaching and now from BGEA is another of His gifts. EvenRidge, our wonderful mountain retreat is really a gift from our parents, and for His work in their lives that allowed them to finish together. And I have only touched the depth of grace poured out on us. We are the recipients of grace for grace the Scripture says. And God asks us simply to give thanks in all things. What do I need that I don't have? And what do I have that I have not been given? Thank you Heavenly Father for Your abundant goodness to us!

Ezekiel 37:1

"The hand of the LORD was on me, and he brought me out by his Spirit and set me down in the middle of the valley; it was full of bones."

This is the famous "dry bones" story made famous by the American spiritual "dem bones, dem bones, dem dry bones". (Read the story in this chapter.) What struck me was the context of this encounter with God. The Spirit was heavy upon this prophet Ezekiel and He brought him to this valley for instruction and revelation. In the Old Testament people sporadically encountered the Holy Spirit in their lives. He came and went, much like the wind. In fact, Jesus used that analogy in John 3, the great chapter that describes being born again. But God has done something different for us. He has enabled His Spirit to live in us.

Do I fully grasp the significance of that? I am a vessel of God's Spirit dwelling in my being!

The second thing I saw in that verse was how the Spirit directed Ezekiel to the work He wanted the prophet to do. The Apostle Paul tells us in Romans 8:14 *"For all those led by God's Spirit are God's sons."* What a privilege to be filled and led by the Holy Spirit! Today invite the indwelling Spirit of God to guide each of your encounters just as He did with Ezekiel in this passage.

John 8:31-32

31 Then Jesus said to the Jews who had believed him, "If you continue in my word, you really are my disciples.
32 You will know the truth, and the truth will set you free."

As I return home from another week on the road, reading God's Word in seat 15d on this American Airlines flight, this verse jumps off the page. Being in God's Word, according to Jesus, is the mark of being His disciple. That should encourage each of us to pursue the Word of God. It can give assurance when doubts creep into the mind. Open the Word. Read its truths. Strengthen your relationship with Christ. The Word is a lamp for guidance and a light for illumination. It shows me truth about God, about myself and about the spiritual world I encounter.

"You will know the truth ". What a wonderful promise. Not "You will know about the truth." But really "know it" so that truth becomes the guiding force of life. An integral part of my thinking and consciousness. Thinking biblically. God's truth set us free. It delivers us from self-deception, the most powerful blinder. It also sheds light when other people throw shade. Being set free from the lies of self and others. And of course the father of lies, our archenemy.

How good that God has provided us His Word. What an excellent gift!

Hebrews 2:1

"For this reason, we must pay attention all the more to what we have heard, so that we will not drift away."

In his training of Tahlon, Jason asks him to "focus".

I have noticed that Tahlon does the same thing to himself when he is drifting on some action or attitude. He reminds himself to "Focus". Being focused on something keeps its importance front and center. It prioritizes and anticipates actions that will follow. Drifting in the spiritual life can lead to sin. By focusing on the person of Christ (for that is the main focus of the Hebrews epistle), my natural drift toward sin can be avoided.

Focus on Jesus today!

Jason and son, Tahlon

$\mathcal{P}salm\ 101{:}3\text{-}4$

3 I will not let anything worthless guide me. I hate the practice of transgression; it will not cling to me.
4 A devious heart will be far from me; I will not be involved with evil.

This passage describes the person who sees clearly the struggle we all face on a moral and ethical level. We constantly encounter transgressions of God's Law, either our own sin or that of others. And sin can cling to us. The Apostle Paul speaks of temptation "seizing" him. Having the right attitude toward unrighteousness is the key starting point for this writer in his struggle against sin. It begins with assigning sin it's true worth. If I think sin has value, it will be harder to reject. In fact, sin is worthless. It steals my joy, my peace, the harmony I might have with others. It interferes in our relationship with a Holy God. Sin's ally in me is a devious heart. Covering up iniquity is the first response of my unregenerate nature; hiding my sin so it won't be revealed or so I might taste from its false pleasure once again. A righteous will and the new heart God gives the redeemed person are the spiritual tools to break this human dilemma. "I <u>will not</u> be involved with evil."

That's a good start especially for the Old Testament believer like this Psalmist. In our day we have a greater ally, the indwelling Holy Spirit Who both illuminates my hidden transgressions and forces them out of my life.

That is what makes the command to "Be holy as I am holy" from our Lord more than mockery or wishful thinking. We have His Presence in and with us this day to reject evil and to live for righteousness. And the starting point ... "I will not".

Another brief thought this morning from the text:

Psalm 102:18 *This will be written for a later generation, and a people who have not yet been created will praise the LORD.*

Whatever we face, the believer has this great hope: we can be a witness to a future generation yet to be born. That might be the impetus to press on in adversity. The future belongs to the godly!

Psalm 135:19-20

19 House of Israel, bless the LORD! House of Aaron, bless the LORD!
20 House of Levi, bless the LORD! You who revere the LORD, bless the LORD!

I would modify this song slightly this morning. House of Greg .. House of Jason .. House of John .. House of Jared, bless the Lord. Reverence the Lord our God. It is the Lord's Day, the day of worship for the Christian. Let's be faithful in seeking the Lord in worship today.

2 Kings 2:23-24

23 From there Elisha went up to Bethel. As he was walking up the path, some small boys came out of the city and jeered at him, chanting, "Go up, baldy! Go up, baldy!"
24 He turned around, looked at them, and cursed them in the name of the LORD. Then two female bears came out of the woods and mauled forty-two of the children.

This incident in the life of Elisha, one of Israel's great prophets has always puzzled me. It contrasts greatly from Jesus' statement, *"Let the little children to come to me for such is the kingdom of God."* Matthew 19:14.

Respect for the Lord was in serious decline in Israel at this time. One of the worst kings, Ahab, had just passed away as had his son. Idolatry was rampant. There was no fear of God. It seems that the sins of leadership inevitably filter down in a society. Having a pack of lawless rascals is the product of such leadership.

The text doesn't say the 42 kids were killed, only mauled by this bear. Some heavy, divine discipline for their disrespectful actions. One wonders if they had ever received correction at home. Possibly not. Praying today for my grandchildren that their parents would effectively train them up in respect, faith and obedience. I certainly would hate to think a black bear in Maggie Valley would need to carry out our duties in their lives!

John 13:34-35

34 "I give you a new command: Love one another. Just as I have
loved you, you are also to love one another.
35 "By this everyone will know that you are my disciples,
if you love one another."

Here is the very essence of the Christian life. Love. For God. For each other. Without this love I cannot claim to be a Jesus follower. Christians have wisdom because we are counseled by the ultimate source of wisdom, the Word taught by the Spirit.

But we aren't known for that. We have knowledge because Christians have traditionally educated their children and promoted education for others.

But we aren't known for that either. The same could be said of righteousness, moderation, humility, courage .. all characteristics of Christian lives through the ages. Yet these don't define Christians. Jesus says there is a single characteristic that marks His people. Love. For God. For each other.

Psalm 108:3-5

A song of praise this Sunday morning.

3 I will praise you, LORD, among the peoples;
I will sing praises to you among the nations.
4 For your faithful love is higher than the heavens,
and your faithfulness reaches to the clouds.
5 God, be exalted above the heavens,
and let your glory be over the whole earth.

My enduring prayer for my grandchildren in **Luke 2:52.**

"And Jesus increased in wisdom and stature, and in favor with God and men."

"God, bring wisdom to each of their minds and hearts, for the fear of the Lord is the beginning of wisdom. And cause them to be physically healthy and strong so they can be defenders and providers as You have designed them to be. And may they have many friends but importantly also have a close friendship with you, O Father. In Jesus name …"

Deuteronomy 6:2

"Do this so that you may fear the LORD your God all the days of your life by keeping all his statutes and commands I am giving you, your son, and your grandson, and so that you may have a long life."

When a person gets to my age (70 is now in the rear view mirror!), one of the things that occupies your thinking is "What will I leave behind?" You begin planning your estate so that heirs will receive something. That is the material side of legacy.

This verse speaks of the spiritual side of legacy and passing on faith in God to generations that will follow. What God gives me in His Word is not just for me, but for Jason, Stacey, John, Jared, Brooke, Tahlon, Ben, Declan, Asa and Rilynn. And even one yet to be born at this writing.

In this verse it is faith that produces obedience to God's commandments. And the reward for that legacy, as the text states, is long life. At my age, living a long life is a truly great reward. Seeing a new generation emerge from infancy to childhood and into adolescence and finally young adulthood is a great blessing. God gives that greatest of gifts to those who fear and obey Him. That is the legacy I want to leave my family. Finishing well the life of faith is the key to leaving a rich inheritance behind. May He grant me the grace and strength to do just that.

Lamentations 2:21-23

21 Yet I call this to mind, and therefore I have hope:
22 Because of the LORD's faithful love we do not perish, for his mercies never end.
23 They are new every morning; great is your faithfulness!

This book by the weeping prophet Jeremiah is surely one of the most depressing in all of Scripture. It details the fall of Judah into the Babylonian captivity. Jeremiah goes into minute detail about how a foreign power breeches the nations defenses (chapter 1), it's impact on people and how the Lord uses this as divine discipline for sin (chapter 2) and the psychological trauma it brings personally to this man of God (verses 1-20 of chapter 3). He is "as low as a mole", as my father used to say.

These are absolutely the worst of times for the nation of Israel and its people like Jeremiah. Yet, in the middle of his national crisis and chaos (and in the very center of his five chapter account) comes this incredible statement of faith and hope. These verses are the scriptural basis for one of my favorite hymns, Great is Thy Faithfulness - also my mother's favorite hymn. I can still hear her beautiful voice singing it. And it makes me tear up. There is nothing we ever face in life that our faith in God cannot overcome. A terrible tragedy, a besetting sin, a hopeless circumstance .. faith in the God of the impossible is all we need to get through to the other side.

Daniel 1:4

"..young men without any physical defect, good-looking, suitable for instruction in all wisdom, knowledgeable, perceptive, and capable of serving in the king's palace."

Raising children is no small task. It is a lengthy process covering years, even decades. And over that time one can lose sight of the goal. Certainly we want our children to be independent and capable of making their own way in the world. But what are those qualities that will best aid them in arriving at that goal? And what should we be instilling in them now that will yield that end? In this description of the young man Daniel, there are four excellent milestones to keep in mind in this awesome and crucial task of raising children. These qualities surfaced in this young man under the most difficult of circumstances, bondage in a foreign land. Yet they enabled him to succeed and even prosper.

1. Wisdom. Here is applied knowledge used in life situations for maximum benefit. A thorough examination of the book of Proverbs offers this.
2. Knowledge. Commitment to learning about their world and how it works. Finding the best educational alternatives and using our home as a classroom for knowledge acquisition.
3. Perceptiveness. Showing our children how to read people and situations, then respond appropriately. This begins with our perceptiveness to them!
4. Servant-spirit. The age we live in trains children in entitlement. Serving others is a greater goal and makes them useful for all kinds of tasks, circumstances and people.

Keep the checklist in your minds as a reference for where these Matthews children are heading under our training.

"Train a child up in the way he should go .."
Proverbs 22:6

Samuel 1: 11

Making a vow, she pleaded, "LORD of Armies, if you will take notice of your servant's affliction, remember and not forget me, and give your servant a son, I will give him to the LORD all the days of his life, and his hair will never be cut."

Prayers and vows to God. That Samuel must have been some guy! His hair was never cut from birth. What a spectacle he would have been walking through the towns and farms of Israel administering justice.

And notice how the childless Hannah addressed God in her prayer - Jehovah Sabbaoth or Lord of Armies. Why didn't she call out to Jehovah Jireh or the One who provides? She desperately wanted God to give her a son.

It made me think about the various ways and names God had revealed Himself to Israel. Because different names of God are often used when calling out to Him in prayer. Here are those names for your prayer life:

- Jehovah Jireh - the LORD provides.
- Jehovah Rapha - the LORD heals.
- Jehovah Nissi - the LORD is a banner of victory.
- Jehovah Mekoddishkem - there LORD sanctifies.
- Jehovah Shalom - the LORD is peace.
- Jehovah Sabbaoth- the LORD of hosts or armies (Hannah's choice of addressing Him in her prayer).
- Jehovah Raah - the LORD is my shepherd (from the great 23d Psalm).
- Jehovah Tsidkenu - the LORD our saving justice used of Him to bring His triumphant reign on earth, the Millenium.

Wonderful names from the Old Testament still appropriate to use in our own day. For God never changes. We pray in Jesus' name, the summation of all those names and we do so mindful of His total ability to hear and answer prayer. Let's be reinforced and renewed in our prayers this day by these awesome names of our God.

John 14

So many great verses in the 14th chapter of John's Gospel to challenge and reward our faith:

6 Jesus told him, "I am the way, the truth, and the life. No one comes to the Father except through me.
15 If you love me, you will keep my commands.
23 Jesus answered, "If anyone loves me, he will keep my word. My Father will love him, and
we will come to him and make our home with him.
27 Peace I leave with you. My peace I give to you.
I do not give to you as the world gives.
Don't let your heart be troubled or fearful.

This is the one that stood out to Gwen this morning as we read in our beautiful mountain home, EvenRidge.

2 "In my Father's house are many rooms;
if not, I would have told you. I am going away to prepare a place for you.

Her thought, "The Lord made us and every animal in creation to need a place. Heaven is not some abstract concept. It fills our deepest needs, and this is one: to have a place that is home."

Ah, the wisdom of a godly wife! And what a wonderful home she has provided me and our children through the years.

Hebrews 7:25

"Therefore, he is able to save completely those who come to God
through him, since he always lives to intercede for them."

Need some assurance in this life? Won't find it in the political sphere. What seemed certain yesterday (free markets) is an open topic today (see socialism in America). How about economy and our finances. That too can change rapidly. Health, relationships all have a frustrating impermanence that makes modern living feel like a journey through a dangerous obstacle course.

It is why we can anchor our souls to this wonderful verse about Jesus. He is able to save us completely. Nothing left incomplete. Nothing that can interfere or cause change of destination. His salvation is certain. And He makes it happen through His great work of prayer. Jesus is at the right hand of the Father praying for you and me. He knows our circumstances, our strengths and weaknesses.

And He knows how to cover it all with Divine intercession. Take a moment to thank Jesus for praying for you today. And ask Him what today's prayer is so you can be part of the answer.

Acts 2:21

"Then everyone who calls on the name of the Lord will be saved."

Here is the great promise of our age. God is a savior.

He is not a judge. Not an avenger. Not a celestial critic.

He doesn't sit up on His heavenly throne and condemn. He saves. And He saves anybody who calls out to Him.

We live in this wonderful age of grace and faith. *"It is by grace you are saved through faith"*. Ephesian 2:8. My choices and actions deserve divine judgment. I cannot run from that.

"The wages of sin is death". Romans 6:23. And I am a confessed sinner. But in this age, the Age of Grace, God the Judge will extend mercy to me and graciously forgive me because Jesus died on the cross and rose again. So I call out to Him. And He saves me from the consequence of my sin.

Let us never forget the unique corner of spiritual history we occupy. We live in the age of God's grace expressed through the atoning work of Jesus Christ. What an amazing blessing! What a wonderful Savior!

1 Peter 1:8-9

8 Though you have not seen him, you love him;
though not seeing him now, you believe in him,
and you rejoice with inexpressible and glorious joy,
9 because you are receiving the goal of your faith, the salvation of your souls.

In Peter's preamble to his letter to first century believers, he reminds them (and us, 2000 years later) of a crucial aspect of salvation. Trusting Jesus Christ as my Savior puts me into relationship with God. That relationship was broken by sin. And in my sinful condition, I faced eternal separation from God. Here Peter captures the emotional side of realizing that in Christ, everything has changed. I am no longer under the penalty of my sin. That should cause rejoicing, in fact "inexpressible and glorious joy".

There can be a ho-hum attitude toward being saved that really is inappropriate. Realizing my eternal situation apart from Christ is essential in receiving Him as my Savior. I am lost apart from Jesus. As Peter says, the goal is that my eternal soul (and condition) will be saved and not be condemned to hell. Now that is cause for celebration, great joy, amazing relief, deepest peace.

Thank You Jesus!!

Zechariah 7

As I watched some of the Brett Kavanaugh Supreme Court hearings yesterday, I was impressed with his knowledge of the law and his wisdom in applying it. This verse in **Zechariah 7** sums up how he came across to me on television:

9 "The LORD of Armies says this: 'Make fair decisions. Show
faithful love and compassion to one another.
10 "Do not oppress the widow or the fatherless, the resident alien or the
poor, and do not plot evil in your hearts against one another.'

The push back against Kavanaugh from the Left was largely focused on his opposition to legal abortion in the nation. But he held firm in his convictions about life as all believers should do. Zechariah gives us good reason to not give into the culture of death in our nation.

Zechariah 12:1 *A declaration of the LORD, who stretched out the heavens, laid the foundation of the earth, and formed the spirit of man within him.*

Imagine! The same act of creating the cosmos is re-done each time a child is formed in the womb. It is on the order of the entire cosmos! So I say to those who refuse to recognize the sanctity of life of the unborn, "open your eyes. Unlock your hearts to his miracle in front of you"

Deuteronomy 19:16-20

16 "If a malicious witness testifies against someone accusing him of a crime,
17 "the two people in the dispute are to stand in the presence of the LORD
before the priests and judges in authority at that time.
18 "The judges are to make a careful investigation, and if the witness
turns out to be a liar who has falsely accused his brother,
19 "you must do to him as he intended to do to his brother. You must purge the evil from you.
20 "Then everyone else will hear and be afraid, and they will
never again do anything evil like this among you.

Isn't it obvious why hoax crimes are on the rise? As a nation we have departed from a biblical worldview with its attendant ethos and morality. We judge criminal behavior not by a dispassionate standard, a code of law but by other factors .. a person's position in society, socio-economic considerations, even their sexual orientation.

In the recent example of Jussie Smollett, his false accusations against a segment of American society should be punished by the same measure as if he had committed that same hate crime. But of course, that will not happen. And as a result, this type of false character assassination will continue to grow and manifest itself in our nation. Departing from the Word of God had serious consequences in Israel. It will have in America, too. It is crucial that as Christians we resist the lawlessness of our culture. We must live by the biblical standard God gave to us. That is one way we can be the salt and light Jesus says we are to be. Despite the changing cultural norms and mores, the Christian remains fixed on a biblical standard and attempts to live up to that.

1 Chronicles 16:10-11

10 Honor his holy name; let the hearts of those who seek the LORD rejoice.
11 Seek the LORD and his strength; seek his face always.

Much to unpack in these two short verses which are part of a longer prayer in the chapter. First, prayer is an honoring of Who God is. He has revealed Himself to us by His name. He was Jehovah in David's time. In our time, we honor God by praying in Jesus' name.

And then this call to seek Him. Seeking the Lord is a heart issue. We do it less with our minds and intellect than with the center of our desire, our hearts. And isn't it true that our reason rarely brings joy. That is a function of emotion, the expression of our hearts.

And what should we seek in Him? His strength (not relying on our own) so that we acknowledge His limitless power and ability. What need do I have that God cannot meet? Can I not trust Him to care for me IN ALL THINGS.

And finally, this seeking after God draws me into relationship with Him. "Seek His face" the prayer says. God is a personal God who expresses Himself. The face is the center of that expression.

A couple weeks ago we were at Jason and Stacey's interacting with the kids. Declan was doing something that Stacey asked him to stop doing. His face made it clear, even when his words failed him, how he would respond. He scrunched up his little eyes, pursed his lips and let it be known how he felt. Our faces reveal our hearts and communicate relational stuff to others. How good to seek the face of God and experience true relationship with Him. Always!

Micah 6:8

"Mankind, he has told each of you what is good and what it is the LORD requires of
you: to act justly, to love faithfulness, and to walk humbly with your God."

We read this wonderful verse at dinner with Scott, Denise, Gwen and John tonight. The godly life is not complicated.

It doesn't require esoteric knowledge. It is transparent before us and powerfully summarized in this verse.

Justice. Mercy. Humility. What more does a person need to please the Lord? In this Holy Week, May we renew commitments to Him and His simple commands for us.

Justice. Mercy. Humility.

2 Chronicles 15

A passage for our dear Asa, whose namesake was a great Judean king and true reformer.

1 The Spirit of God came on Azariah son of Oded.
2 So he went out to meet Asa and said to him, "Asa and all Judah and Benjamin,
hear me. The LORD is with you when you are with him. If you seek him, he
will be found by you, but if you abandon him, he will abandon you.
8 When Asa heard these words and the prophecy of Azariah son of Oded the prophet,
he took courage and removed the abhorrent idols from the whole land of Judah and
Benjamin and from the cities he had captured in the hill country of Ephraim.

Asa took courage and acted. And his actions were those of a righteous follower of the true God. He turned to God and not away from Him. He sought Him and the righteousness revealed in the Law of Moses. And God did not abandon Asa. And he won't abandon us as we seek Him and follow His commands.

The Lord will never abandon you, dear Asa Robert Matthews, as you seek Him and follow Him in your life.

Psalm 127:3-5

The text we had this morning with Scott and Denise.

So appropriate for these two couples as we count the many blessings the Lord has poured over us.

3 Behold, children are a heritage from the LORD, the fruit of the womb a reward.
4 Like arrows in the hand of a warrior are the children of one's youth.
5 Blessed is the man who fills his quiver with them!
He shall not be put to shame when he speaks with his enemies in the gate.

Deuteronomy 30:19-20

19 "I call heaven and earth as witnesses against you today that I have set before you life
and death, blessing and curse. Choose life so that you and your descendants may live,
20 "love the LORD your God, obey him, and remain faithful to him. For he is your life,
and he will prolong your days as you live in the land the LORD swore to give to your
fathers Abraham, Isaac, and Jacob."

This morning I apologize for going political rather than devotional. Gwen and I saw the new film Unplanned last night. It is a powerful production and one that is being suppressed by the mainstream media who promote the abortion industry in our nation. I have heard that Twitter and Facebook have lifted ads for the film. Choosing life, as this verse calls on God's people to do has a very contemporary and concrete application. For the Israelites, it meant choosing to obey and serve God, their source of life and vitality. It was a spiritual call to being faithful. The previous chapter outlines the harsh consequences of failure to obey God, to choose the life He offers.

In our context, this film reveals a similar ultimatum. In choosing to allow and to even promote the destruction of life in the womb, we have fostered a culture of death. We kill the most helpless and ourselves reap the fruit of that crime. Our nation is divided. Our culture is in chaos.

Our land is under siege. We suffer afflictions both physical and emotional.

We are dying. The warnings outlined by Moses in this prescient text have come down on this nation because we have chosen death. It is imperative that Christians are outspoken proponents of life. We must be salt (preservative) and light (illumination) in our darkened world. We must defend the unborn and oppose every attempt to destroy them. The future of our offspring is dependent on our obedience. There can be no compromise with the abortion industry and their advocates. We must choose life!

Psalm 119:89

89 LORD, your word is forever; it is firmly fixed in heaven.

(My father often quoted this verse. It was why he memorized so much scripture).

105 Your word is a lamp for my feet and a light on my path.

(One of the first verses I learned as a child and taught my kids)

114 You are my shelter and my shield; I put my hope in your word.
130 The revelation of your words brings light and gives understanding to the inexperienced.

(A verse my grandad helped me learn.)

140 Your word is completely pure, and your servant loves it.
160 The entirety of your word is truth, each of your righteous judgments endures forever.
165 Abundant peace belongs to those who love your instruction; nothing makes them stumble.

(One of Grandma Lou's favorite verses).

Three generations of our family impacted by the Word of God. Now a fourth (my sons and daughters) and hopefully a fifth to encounter the living and abiding Word of God.

1 Chronicles 15:7

"But as for you, be strong; don't give up, for your work has a reward."

Today this verse jumped off the page. Be strong. Don't give up. Your work has a reward. Marriage is hard work. Blending two separate personalities into a one (the two become one, as Scripture says) is not a Sunday walk in the park. There are challenges and conflicts. It is difficult. Maybe that is what makes a long term marriage such a great reward. I value few things more than Gwen. It wasn't always that way. But sometime around the 15th year of marriage she surpassed Duck football in my estimation. (That's mostly a joke!)

And what about raising kids. That needs endurance. Strength. Persistence. But when you get to this stage of grand parenting, all of it takes on new meaning. It bridges from the immediate present to the future hope a family can give. That's a unique perspective that only comes through work, persistence and refusing to give up. There is a great reward in seeing your children raising their children.

Career. Serving the Lord. Neighborliness. The list can go on. Strength. Persistence. Reward. Excellent advice for a fulfilling life

Daniel 9:4

4 I prayed to the LORD my God and confessed:
Ah, Lord — the great and awe-inspiring God who keeps
his gracious covenant with those who love him and keep his commands —
5 we have sinned, done wrong, acted wickedly, rebelled, and turned away from your
commands and ordinances. And notice how this prayer of repentance is received by God.
23 "At the beginning of your petitions an answer went out, and I
have come to give it, for you are treasured by God."

This is great comfort to a repentant sinner. It is true that sin breaks our relationship with a holy God. Unconfessed sin will remove Him from us forever. But God has made the provision for us to deal with our transgressions. In the time of the Old Testament, sacrifices were offered for sin. But Jesus, the

Lamb of God, is our sacrifice for sin. His blood cleanses the repentant sinner from the consequence of iniquity. He alone restores our relationship with a holy God. And what a note of assurance in this 23rd verse; God treasures us. That is why He made a way to return to Him.

"For God so loved the world that He gave His one and only Son ..." John 3:16

Take a moment right now to thank Him for Jesus. And if any sin comes to mind, repent and receive His forgiveness. Start this day clean and forgiven before God. He treasures you.

Daniel 12:4

One other nugget from the final chapter of Daniels amazing prophecy.

"But you, Daniel, keep these words secret and seal the book until the time of the end.
Many will roam about, and knowledge will increase."

He is speaking here about the end of the age when God brings human history to a grand, climactic conclusion.

And the two things Daniel foretells are two things so evident in our day access to travel, access to information.

Has there ever been an age like the present one when people can roam the earth so freely.

Jared and Brooke are nearly a third of the way around the earth this morning in the Hawaiian Islands. And we are discussing these biblical truths with them! These are truly the last days that Daniel described.

Jared and Brooke, Hawaii, 2019

Psalm 106:21

21 They forgot God their Savior, who did great things in Egypt,
22 wondrous works in the land of Ham, awe-inspiring acts at the Red Sea.
23 So he said he would have destroyed them — if Moses his chosen one had not stood
before him in the breach to turn his wrath away from destroying them.

Here is one, Moses, who stood in the gap for his people. Without his intercession, Israel would have been disavowed by God and destroyed. Their idolatry and disobedience had broken the relationship with their Redeemer. Can that happen with us? Is there a point that we can alienate Jesus so that it threatens are eternal well-being, our salvation? I'm not sure I have that definitive answer. But I am sure there is always a need for someone to stand in the gap for me, someone to plead my case before the Judge of all the earth. And there is one in heaven Who does just that; Jesus Christ our high priest. And there are others in the body of Christ who do it too. Gap-standers. People who persistently plead my case before God. Phineas was such a man in Israel.

Psalm 106:30 *But Phinehas stood up and intervened, and the plague was stopped.*
31 It was credited to him as righteousness throughout all generations to come.

What a promise to the gap-stander! Having an eternal account of righteousness and not only for him, but for those to follow in his family as well. I want to be one of those Phineas-types who stands in the gap for my children, grandchildren and others who pleads their case before God. Care to join me?

Ezra 1:5

"So the family heads of Judah and Benjamin, along with the priests and Levites — everyone whose spirit God had roused — prepared to go up and rebuild the LORD's house in Jerusalem."

That phrase - everyone whose spirit God had roused - got me thinking this morning. How does God stir us? And how sensitive am I to the prompting of God in my life? In our present era, the Church

Age, we have a most unique relationship with God that enables Him to speak, guide and chasten us: the indwelling Holy Spirit. This is a truly unique relationship no other previous age of history has experienced. God has made us His temple where He exists and through whom He works. As I respond to the Spirit's guidance and prompting in my life, His ability to "rouse" me, to get my attention becomes more acute. Conversely, my ignorance of His leading can quench His work in my life, setting me at odds with His purposes. The Holy Spirit can direct all kinds of actions as I am listening to His direction - job change, caring for sickness, providing for family and friends are just some things we have prayed for recently in our family. These requests have been acted on by the indwelling Holy Spirit who is full of grace and mercy. Also, the Spirit molds our characters according to nine wonderful qualities He possesses: love, joy, peace, patience, goodness, kindness, gentleness, faithfulness, self-control. What an amazing Presence to have in my life as I encounter all the things I will face this day.

Zephaniah 1:6

".. and those who turn back from following the LORD, who do not seek the LORD or inquire of him."

This passage expresses God's extreme displeasure and judgment. And His chosen, covenant people are not excluded from that judgment. From the divine perspective, there is no "neutral" in the spiritual gearbox. Either I am moving forward in relationship with God or reversing back to attitudes and practices I once possessed. Evidence of that reversal is mentioned in two ways. No seeking after God. No prayer life.

Seeking Him in its most basic sense is having a God-consciousness in daily life. It is living with Him in my thoughts and actions rather than absent from Him. I can believe in God but live as a functional agnostic by never including Him in my Decision-making, my choices, my worldview .. basically my awareness. Inquiring of God, as the text says, is prayer. Conversing with the Almighty. Such a blessing and privilege. But do I engage him in that conversation of faith? Do I appreciate His abiding presence? Do I admit my shortcomings or seek His counsel and wisdom? God opened the door wide to a personal relationship with us. He sought us out. But relationship requires response. It is a two-way street.

What will my relationship with God look like today?

Job 11:6

"He would show you the secrets of wisdom, for true wisdom has two sides.
Know then that God has chosen to overlook some of your iniquity."

A statement from one of Job's "friends" attempting to get him to admit that Job's hidden iniquity is the cause of his suffering. But the statement has some real truth in it (even if not applied to Job). Isn't it true that there are two sides to most conflicts? And that by being stuck on my own perspective, I am unable to perceive the other person's point of view? How often I have been blinded by what I felt and ignored Gwen's feelings? Wouldn't it be wiser to probe a little to find her side of the issue? Wouldn't that facilitate better understanding and foster a more loving relationship?

It could be the same for parent/child conflicts. I like the way my daughter-in-laws probe their children's issues before arriving at a course of discipline (I'm sure Jared and Jason do the same). Could be a wet diaper, a hunger pain, a difficult relationship at school. Another side to the behavior that more fully explains it.

And think of that last phrase, God overlooking iniquity. In the balance of divine judgment, God takes into consideration both the righteous and the unrighteousness in our lives. Good to know that He sees both sides and is slow to anger.

Ephesians 4: 1-3

Look at the Apostle Paul's inspired instruction for keeping a family (or any group) together.

1 Therefore I, the prisoner for the Lord, urge you to walk worthy of the calling you have received,
2 with all humility and gentleness, with patience, accepting one another in love,
3 diligently keeping the unity of the Spirit with the peace that binds us.

Here is the secret to family life from the biblical perspective - humility, gentleness, patience, acceptance in love with the ultimate outcome of peace. Praying for all of you, family!

Psalm 136

1 Give thanks to the LORD, for he is good. His faithful love endures forever.
26 Give thanks to the God of heaven! His faithful love endures forever.

In this 136th Psalm, every verse from first to last concludes with the phrase, "His faithful love endures forever." It is an obvious point of emphasis this song writer wanted to make. Faithfulness and love.. enduring attributes. And paired together, one of the greatest descriptions of our God. Faithfulness is a necessary component of love. We live in an age when love is expressed in a fleeting, sensual way. But this writer underscores again and again that true love necessarily requires faithfulness. It is why we vow at the marriage ceremony "as long as we both shall live." That is the expression of our intent to combine faithfulness to the love being expressed for our spouse. A modern version of the marriage vow (as long as we both shall <u>love</u>) strips away that necessary foundation of true, godly love and trivializes the vow. Love and faithfulness are inextricably bound. That is why the psalmist writes with such certainty about this love enduring. It is real love. It is grounded in the character of God Himself. And it is offered to each of us who recognize its value and power. "We love because He first loved us."

We attended the wedding ceremony of a dear friend yesterday who lost her spouse to cancer five years ago. Sue was only 55 when Charlie died. As I witnessed the exchange of her new vows with Todd, great emotion welled up in me. I cried without restraint. So thankful for witnessing the conclusion of a faithful love. Charlie and Sue had finished their vows to each other. And at the same time the formation of a new commitment to faithful love. I squeezed Gwen's hand with deepest gratitude. God was in that room overseeing the ceremony. It was His enduring, faithful love we witnessed and rejoiced in. Not just for Sue and Todd. But for us, too.

"Give thanks to the God of heaven! His faithful love endures forever."

James 3: 17-18

17 But the wisdom from above is first pure, then peace-loving, gentle, compliant,
full of mercy and good fruits, unwavering, without pretense.
18 And the fruit of righteousness is sown in peace by those who cultivate peace.

Two of the best character verses in all scripture. Who doesn't want to be wise? Here the effects of wisdom are discussed. 8 wonderful character traits. Can you find them?

1.

2.

3.

4.

5.

6.

7.

8.

Jeremiah 4: 14

"O Jerusalem, wash your heart from wickedness, That you may be saved.
How long shall your evil thoughts lodge within you?"

Consider how our minds and thoughts operate. This verse gives me a great challenge to guard them. Wickedness can take root in my thoughts. It can gain a foothold not easily dislodged. Sinful thinking and meditating on unrighteousness seems to become a pattern .. if I allow it. It is the condition of the natural man and the unredeemed mind.

In Christ, I am offered freedom from this cycle of evil reflection. In Him, God plants truth and righteousness on my heart and mind, giving me the way of escape from that vicious cycle and then an ongoing maintenance that permits godly, lifestyle thinking.

Paul had that latter thing in mind in the great Romans 12 passage: 2 *"And do not be conformed to this world, but be transformed by the renewing of your mind, that you may prove what is that good and acceptable and perfect will of God."*

Renewal is a choice offered to me by His grace this day. "Lord, let me not wallow in unrighteous thought, but renew my mind this day that the light of Your Word may guide my thoughts."

1 Cor 15:54-57

An Easter Devotional
Death is swallowed up in victory."
"O death, where is your victory?
O death, where is your sting?"
The sting of death is sin, and the
power of sin is the law.
But thanks be to God,
who gives us the victory
through our Lord Jesus Christ.

I made my decision to follow Jesus Christ on Easter Sunday, 1981. It was the culmination of seeking a relationship with God I wanted since He had revealed Himself to me nearly year before. He had shown me He was real and present as I lay in bed wrestling with many poor life choices. His revelation came in a verse of Scripture: *"Trust in the Lord."* (Proverbs 3:5)

It took Gwen and me a year of visiting churches before finding a little church in Northeast

Portland where the gospel was plainly preached and repentance and faith in Jesus Christ offered as the only means of salvation. I took the offer. And my life has never been the same since.

"Thank you Father, for sending Your only begotten Son to be our Savior."

Joshua 1:6-9

6 *"Be strong and of good courage, for to this people you shall divide as an inheritance the land which I swore to their fathers to give them.*
7 *"Only be strong and very courageous, that you may observe to do according to all the law which Moses My servant commanded you ..*
8 *"This Book of the Law shall not depart from your mouth, but you shall meditate in it day and night, that you may observe to do according to all that is written in it ..*
9 *"Have I not commanded you? Be strong and of good courage; do not be afraid, nor be dismayed, for the LORD your God is with you wherever you go."*

Four areas of strength and courage God calls us to:

Verse 6 - to be strong on His promises. Don't waiver from the things God has promised. He is faithful. He will do it.

Verse 7 – be strong in obedience. The promises of God and commands of God are linked. As I am strong in one, the other seems to follow.

Verse 8 – be strong in the Word. As His Word takes a preeminent place in my life, His promises and commands are integral to my thinking.

Verse 9. Strong in my emotions. How often this is the area - some have called it "soulishness" - that interferes with the walk of faith described in 6-8. I must take mood swings under the control of my faith, His Word and promises so the latter things determine my emotional state.

Matthew 8:2

And behold, a leper came and worshiped Him, saying, "Lord, if You are willing, You can make me clean."

Answer: Always!

In the 5th chapter of John, Jesus has another encounter with a crippled man. He turns the question around!

> *6 When Jesus saw him lying there, and knew that he already had been in that condition a long time, He said to him, "Do you want to be made well?"*

That is the more telling question for us. Not whether God is willing to heal us, but if we are willing to have our ailments removed. Sure, I always want my physical infirmities healed. Who wouldn't? But what about the moral and spiritual ones? Do I really want His salvation from those?

Perhaps I become too settled in my sin and iniquity even to the point of enjoying it. He is always willing and able to make me whole.

The question is, am I willing to be healed?

Genesis 11:1-9

> *1 Now the whole earth had one language and one speech.*
> *2 And it came to pass, as they journeyed from the east, that they found a plain in the land of Shinar, and they dwelt there.*
> *3 Then they said to one another, "Come, let us make bricks and bake them thoroughly." They had brick for stone, and they had asphalt for mortar.*
> *4 And they said, "Come, let us build ourselves a city, and a tower whose top is in the heavens; let us make a name for ourselves, lest we be scattered abroad over the face of the whole earth."*
> *5 But the LORD came down to see the city and the tower which the sons of men had built.*

6 And the LORD said, "Indeed the people are one and they all have one language, and this is what they begin to do; now nothing that they propose to do will be withheld from them.
7 "Come, let Us go down and there confuse their language, that
they may not understand one another's speech."
8 So the LORD scattered them abroad from there over the face
of all the earth, and they ceased building the city.
9 Therefore its name is called Babel, because there the LORD confused the language of all the earth; and from there the LORD scattered them abroad over the face of all the earth.

Some thoughts on this interesting epoch of human history:

1. Communication is a defining difference of human beings and the rest of the animal world. (Verse 1) and enables man to employ ever greater technologies to adapt to- and control his environment (verse 3).
2. That adaption and technology often flies directly in the face of God's will for mankind in the world He created for us (verse 4). It reveals the fundamental spiritual problem we face of our sin nature rebelling against Gods will.
3. God recognizes the incredible capacities He created in us and their potential for both good and evil. (Verse 6)
4. Part of Gods redemptive plan is to frustrate our rebellion so that His grace is enabled in our lives. (Verse 7).

Good to check on the frustrations of life to see if perhaps God is speaking to me about whether I am following His will or off on my own tangent like the ancient civilization of Babel on the plain of Shinar.

Romans 15:13

One of my favorite verses from **Romans 15** today, one I would like read at my funeral (whenever it happens).

13 Now may the God of hope fill you with all joy and peace in believing,
that you may abound in hope by the power of the Holy Spirit.

First, Paul says faith (or here referred to as believing) will produce joy and peace. That is the stuff that makes life pleasant. Who doesn't want to live in joy and in peace?

Well, test your faith. It should be yielding those priceless qualities of life.

With joy and peace as a foundation, I become a person of hope. That is because the source of hope (the God of hope as the text says) delivers these prized qualities through His grace and His abiding Spirit. And His hope is further amplified by the fruit of faith, namely joy and peace.

So consider this amazing triad ... hope, joy, peace. What is truly better than a life in Christ? I have sought many sources for these three qualities of life. But only in Jesus have I found them.

1 Corinthians 1:8

8 He will also strengthen you to the end, so that you will be blameless in the day of our Lord Jesus Christ. 9 God is faithful; you were called by him into fellowship with his Son, Jesus Christ our Lord.

Who wants to meet the Lord with a pile of sins and wrongdoing still stacked on their life account? Not me. The problem is, those sins still seem to pile up. I truly wish they did not, but I remain a sinner after all these years of knowing and serving Christ.

Wretched man that I am! Paul sure had me in his sights with that comment from Romans 7. But the Great Apostle also has us pictured in these comments. And that is a great consolation. Strengthened to be blameless on the day of Christ Jesus.

The order of that instruction is crucial. I need strength in the struggle against iniquity. If I'm ever to be blameless, as the verse implies, I need inner transformation every time my flesh opts for evil.

That is where the faithfulness of God enters this spiritual/moral equation. He will not rest or give up on my pursuit of holiness of standing blameless before Him in that day. It is the only means of fellowship with a holy God. And He is absolutely committed to the task. So committed He sent His Son on a rescue mission that required death and resurrection.

So I am not in despair. And I am not yielding to the dark presences in my life. I can't ignore them. Can't wish them away. But I can trust a faithful God to bring about His ultimate purposes in my life - blamelessness to fellowship with Him in that final day.

Psalm 117:8

"For you, LORD, rescued me from death, my eyes from tears, my feet from stumbling."

Here is the total sufficiency of the Lord and why He can be trusted completely. He protects me from the greatest physical trial .. death. He delivers from emotional trauma.. my tears. He guides me through my moral quandary, the spiritual stuff .. stumbling. See how perfect is the salvation of our God.

He covers my body, soul and spirit. *"Trust in the Lord with all your heart."* Proverbs 3:5

1 Corinthians 2:5-6

"That your faith should not be in the wisdom of men but in the power of God."

The Matthews family loves a good argument. We enjoy arranging facts, causation and rhetorical devices to convince each other of politics, sports and religion. We even take on culture at times. As a proponent of this, my tendency is to pursue Christian apologetics that confirm the veracity of my faith. Apologetics is a good thing for Christians to study. It confirms and reinforces belief. It builds a powerful perimeter around the encroaching rationalistic and false doctrines of our age. But as Paul asserts here, a good argument is insufficient to win someone to faith in Christ. I believe in Jesus Christ not because it was the best argument or the most reasonable course to follow. I believe because He revealed His story - the Gospel - to me in a little Northeast Portland church on Easter, 1981. And at that moment all the arguments, reasons and explanations I had built up over the years faded under the brightness of this one truth: Jesus died for my sin .. rose again for my justification .. and will come again to judge the living and the dead.

6 However, we speak wisdom among those who are mature, yet not the wisdom of this age, nor of the rulers of this age, who are coming to nothing.

Matthew 13:22

"Now he who received seed among the thorns is he who hears the word, and the cares of this world and the deceitfulness of riches choke the word, and he becomes unfruitful."

Two things that can choke the impact of God's Word in my life; worry and wealth. Worry robs me of an active prayer life; faith-filled, ongoing conversation with God. As Paul said,

"Don't worry about anything, but in everything, through prayer and petition with thanksgiving; present your requests to God." Philippians 4:6

Wealth can steal my dependence and gratitude toward God. If I rely too much on my bank account or 401K and not the One who provides those things, I lose touch with the true source of my provisions. Better to simply adhere to Jesus' teaching of ask, seek and knock.

"Ask, and it will be given to you. Seek, and you will find. Knock, and the door will be opened to you." Matthew 7:7

The fruit of this life will be gratitude and contentment.

Genesis 18:10

10 And He said, "I will certainly return to you according to the time of life, and behold, Sarah your wife shall have a son." (Sarah was listening in the tent door which was behind him.)
11 Now Abraham and Sarah were old, well advanced in age; and Sarah had passed the age of childbearing.
12 Therefore Sarah laughed within herself, saying, "After I have grown old, shall I have pleasure, my lord being old also?"

13 ¶ And the LORD said to Abraham, "Why did Sarah laugh, saying, 'Shall I surely
bear a child, since I am old?' 14 "Is anything too hard for the LORD? At the appointed
time I will return to you, according to the time of life, and Sarah shall have a son."
15 ¶ But Sarah denied it, saying, "I did not laugh," for she was
afraid. And He said, "No, but you did laugh!

Here is an instructive encounter between the Lord and Sarah (and by application, each of us.). God visited Abraham and Sarah to affirm His covenant with them that He would make their offspring into a great nation. This at a time when Sarah was long past child bearing age.

Her response was so relatable: "Right! It ain't gonna happen, not at my age." Muttered either under her breath or in that inner conversation we often have with ourselves. God knows even these most private thoughts. Nothing is hidden from Him. He knows my doubts, my fears, my lusts, my anger .. all the things I keep bottled up. And He isn't afraid to call me out. I can identify with Sarah's response to being exposed. Denial and minimizing rather than acknowledgment and confession. "I didn't do it" or "It isn't that bad". Better to fess' up, ask forgiveness and simply believe the voice of God rather than the voices in my head.

~~

Joshua 22:26-27

26 Therefore we said, 'Let us now prepare to build ourselves an
altar, not for burnt offering nor for sacrifice,
27 'but that it may be a witness between you and us and our generations after us,
that we may perform the service of the LORD before Him with our burnt offerings,
with our sacrifices, and with our peace offerings; that your descendants may not
say to our descendants in time to come, "You have no part in the LORD."

An interesting event in the history of the twelve tribes. 2 and 1/2 tribes were allotted land on the east side of the Jordan away from the land of the other tribes to the west. This altar of stones was set up to commemorate that so no future misunderstanding would arise about the standing of these eastern tribes vis a vis the Lord and their other brethren.

I was thinking about a similar memorial in our lives that marks us as followers of Christ, firmly committed to serve Him, as that memorial altar represented in Israel. For us it is baptism. On that day and in those waters we make a public declaration about our faith and intention to be followers of Jesus Christ, identifying with Him in His death and resurrection.

I remember so clearly my baptism in the pool of a little church in Northeast Portland and the older brother who baptized me as a follower of Christ. Two months later Gwen along with her sister and husband entered those same waters of witness to declare their faith in Christ. That was 1981. Within a couple more years Jason was baptized in that same pool at Laurel Park Bible Chapel. After our church moved to Clackamas and we built Spring Mountain, I had the honor of baptizing Jared one Sunday in the early 1990s. Then a few years later, after we had moved to North Carolina (I think it was 2004) I baptized John in a swimming pool in Davidson, a few days before he headed to boot camp in the Marine corps.

What important times to remember as memorials to our faith and intentions! And as this next generation of Matthews children grow up and declare their faith in Christ, it will be a joy to lay down these memorial, symbolic altars .. life-defining decisions that witness to others of their faith in Jesus Christ and their intention to be His followers.

Isaiah 25: 1

"O LORD, You are my God. I will exalt You, I will praise Your name, For You have done wonderful things; Your counsels of old are faithfulness and truth."

The great prophet brings us a charge this morning to worship and give thanks to our God. The reason? All the wonderful things He has done. Consider creation and the fullness and beauty of this world. I love the program Planet Earth as it shows the myriad ways God fashioned this world for us to enjoy.

Then consider His redemptive acts that express His care and love. How He made a way for our salvation from the consequence of sin by shedding His own blood on the cross. How He forgives us in Christ and teaches us to forgive each other.

And what about the way God sustains us. He provides what we need as an expression of His faithfulness. He is a kind and compassionate deity, actively engaged with our needs. With Isaiah we can say, "I will exalt and praise the name of the Lord my God. Truly He has done wonderful things."

Psalm 145:4

"One generation will declare your works to the next and will proclaim your mighty acts."

Here is a charge for all parents and grandparents. It is a command to express the greatness and goodness of God to our children/grandchildren. The testimony of one generation to the next is a crucial part of transmitting the faith generationally.

So I ask myself: "Have I told my three sons adequately of how God transformed my life in 1981? Do they know about the way the gospel swept through our family in that miraculous spring and summer and changed lives, marriages, homes? Have they ever seen the image of a little church in northeast Portland having two complete rows filled with the Matthews and Evans families on Sunday morning at the Breaking of Bread? Do they understand how addictions, immorality, despair were instantly replaced with hope, righteousness and salvation?

That was the mighty act of God in this family those many years ago. It needs to be told and re-told lest we forget and fail to give our Savior, the Lord Jesus Christ the praise He is due. And to keep alive the reality of salvation and life-change Christ alone can bring.

Psalm 139: 13-14

13 For it was you who created my inward parts; you knit me together in my mother's womb.
14 I will praise you because I have been remarkably and wondrously
made. Your works are wondrous, and I know this very well.

My mind focuses this morning on a yet to be born child in our family. What a miracle, this new life coming into our midst. Today's passage extols that miracle. Fearfully and wonderfully made the Psalmist writes.

God's hand shaping our very being is the theme. It elicits worship. We are not creatures of chance. Our existence is not a random act. We are personally crafted by God. He is infinitely creative. No two of us are exactly the same. We bear commonalities. But we are also totally unique - no clones in God's creation.

The rights of each individual is the basis of our cultural experience as Americans. From this we understand human rights and responsibilities, all endowed by our Creator. And this newest addition to the human family (and to our family) will be the same. A completely, never-before-seen person fashioned by the gracious Hand of God. Rights endowed by his creator. Responsibilities to use all his gifts to the glory of God. The same for each one of us. Let us never cease to defend the rights of the unborn.

Habakkuk 1:7

"They are fierce and terrifying; their views of justice and sovereignty stem from themselves."

The prophet is referring to the antecedents of the Babylonians, the nation that rose to world dominance and enslaved Israel in the 6th century BC. It struck me that the prophet identifies the source of this culture's matchless power and brutality to subjugate the world in this era: that their ethics, their law, their power were self-derived. The Babylonians did not submit to God for their legitimacy. They were not guided by any type of divine revelation or will. There were no Ten Commandments to limit their power. Thus, they were a cruel, brutal people who acted out of the overflow of their own corrupt hearts.

Fast forward a couple thousand years to our times. And apply the same principle to modern leftist movements - Mao in China, Hitler in Germany, Lenin/Stalin in Russia. The list goes on: Pol Pot, Castro, Chavez. These are all modern leftists who reject the notion of divine revelation, natural law, man subject to God that are the foundations of our Constitutional system. Justice and legitimacy were all derived from their own evil machinations and their ideologies. It is the basic reason why the left cannot be allowed into power in this or any other country. The left becomes a law unto itself, the ends justifying the means, the state used to accomplish whatever the issue du jour requires.

Acts 20:21

"I testified to both Jews and Greeks about repentance toward God and faith in our Lord Jesus."

Here is the great Apostle's gospel message in brief summation. The message is universal for all people, here described as Jews and Gentiles. It is the fulfillment of one of the oldest promises of God, that Abraham would be a spiritual light to the entire world.

I have had the privilege of traveling to more than 80 countries primarily to represent the Gospel of Christ. It truly is the unique and universal message for all people everywhere. There is nothing like it. That message is two-fold and profound. First faith in the finished work of Jesus. He died for our sins because God so loved the world. In bearing our sins on the cross, the door (He is also that door!) to eternal life and relationship with a holy God is opened. Faith in Christ.

But also repentance. Paul's message is not an add-on to how we are already living. It is not the latest, greatest scheme to make us feel better about ourselves. It is a change in direction (repentance), a radical restructure. The Gospel is given to people who want not only a new start but also a new birth.

Repentance, faith for whosoever will: the Gospel message of Paul and the one for us today. Has it changed your life?

Matthew 16:26

"For what profit is it to a man if he gains the whole world, and loses his own soul?
Or what will a man give in exchange for his soul?"

Here is Jesus putting my priorities back in line. How much concern do I place on the most valuable? I regularly monitor the 401k. I keep close tabs on my savings and checking. I replace the oil in my car and keep up with my home repairs. How vital to also tend (or perhaps first attend) to the condition of my soul and my relationship with Jesus Christ. That is what will extend into the life to come.

Make a list of the things standing between you and the Lord today:

"Lord, give me a renewed vision of the condition of my soul this day. And let Your Word nourish and correct where needed."

Proverbs 20:1

"Wine is a mocker, beer is a brawler; whoever goes astray because of them is not wise."

I had to chuckle when I read this today. Wine produces one type of behavior, beer another it would seem. In the case of beer, think of a tavern brawl. Aggressive dudes taking on the slightest insult. As a substance, it is the longshoremen cultural beverage.

Wine, on the other hand, is for the cultural elite. Think upper Manhattan: the In Crowd. And it produces the cynic. Under its influence I retreat into self-adulation, certain of my correct analysis of all problems, griefs and woes.

The critic versus the brawler. The fact is, substances produce changes in my character. I don't desire either of those outcomes. But when alcohol is consumed over time and quantity, Proverbs warns that I can't avoid these consequences. Presently, I'm on an alcohol vacation. I like to do this at least yearly. I put the beer and wine away on a top shelf and let them age awhile. It gives me perspective on the role these potentially harmful substances play in my life. I want to control these beverages, not be controlled by them. Because, as Solomon points out, there are behavioral outcomes when I overuse beer and wine. My break from them gives me an annual metric of the role they play. I need that correction to insure I'm not heading into alcohol dependency. Maybe you need it, too.

2 Chronicles 1:10

*"Now grant me wisdom and knowledge so that I may lead these
people, for who can judge this great people of yours?"*

Solomon's prayer to God after he took the reins of power in Israel. What a selfless, wise prayer. He has been given a huge responsibility .. to lead a nation at the very apex of its power and influence. Israel never had been or never would be again the nation it became under King David, Solomon's father. And this new king knew he needed help from Yahweh to accomplish his mission.

Don't we need a similar answered prayer from God? We have been given the important task of leading families. God invites us to ask, seek and knock for our needs. Let's seek the wisdom and grace needed to raise our children in the ways they are meant to go. Let's be attentive to each of their special abilities, always pointing them to the One who has made provision for their souls by His blood shed on the cross. And let's model the life of faith so they can see the great doctrines of the Bible fleshed out in the people closest to them.

2 Chronicles 20:12

Here is a great prayer to consider offering to God in times of confusion and uncertainty.

"Our God, will you not judge them? For we are powerless before this vast number that comes to fight against us. We do not know what to do, but we look to you."

"We do not know what to do, but we look to you."

How often in our lives is this the exact case. In this situation, King Jehoshaphat faced a foreign army that seemed impossible to defeat. He lacked the resources, both human and material to dislodge this invasion force. And he was left with prayer alone.

How often God invites us into difficult circumstances that test our faith. If we could handle the situation, we would hardly need prayer and His help. But that is exactly why He permitted this to happen to Jehoshaphat, so the king would turn to his God and his deliverer. Our difficulties might not be as profound as this king's were. But in confusing and difficult times, God invites us to cry out with the same prayer of Jehoshaphat .. "Lord, we do not know what to do, but we look to you."

2 Chronicles 26:16

"But when he became strong, he grew arrogant, and it led to his own destruction."

This is said of the Israelite king Uzziah, who led the nation during the life of the great prophet Isaiah. Uzziah had been a reformer who turned Israel back from idolatry. He started well. But, as often happened in the history of Judah's kings, he finished poorly.

I think of the Proverb, *"Pride goes before a fall, a haughty spirit before destruction."* Proverbs 16:18.

This king was the classic example of that. It was the same character flaw that his father Amaziah failed in. In fact, so many of these kings walked away from the Lord at the height of their success.

What a lesson for us! I love to see success, both in my efforts and also in my family. But success brings a cautionary note .. it can produce self-satisfaction, pride and finally arrogance. Better to simply be thankful, maintain a humble spirit and return the praise to God. He is the One who enabled this Israelite king to succeed, no different than in our lives.

2 Chronicles 30:9

"For when you return to the LORD, your brothers and your sons will receive mercy in the presence of their captors and will return to this land. For the LORD your God is gracious and merciful; he will not turn his face away from you if you return to him."

It was a time of national repentance in Israel. The places of idolatry had been destroyed. The worship of Yahweh restored in the temple. Priests and Levites were consecrated to the Lord. The people re-dedicated themselves to following and serving God. As a nation, Israel needed a spiritual renewal. And it had happened.

We are no different. Our tendency is to be unfaithful to God at times. We do what we should not do and fail to do what we should. Not unlike the Israelites of the 6th century BC. Some things never change. Good to know that God doesn't change either. He won't follow us into sin. He will always set the righteous standard. But He will be merciful and gracious when we come back to Him with all our hearts. As the text says, "He will not turn His face away." And He will restore us.

"Lord, we turn our faces back to You and away from those things that offend You, grateful for Your mercy that forgives us and sets our course anew."

Acts 16:27

27 When the jailer woke up and saw the doors of the prison standing open, he drew his sword and was going to kill himself, since he thought the prisoners had escaped.

28 But Paul called out in a loud voice, "Don't harm yourself, because we're all here!"
29 The jailer called for lights, rushed in, and fell down trembling before Paul and Silas.
30 He escorted them out and said, "Sirs, what must I do to be saved?"
31 They said, "Believe in the Lord Jesus, and you will be saved — you and your household."

I love biblical testimonies of God's power and grace.

An earthquake had opened the doors of this first century Roman prison and broken the chains of the prisoners. How can an earthquake break chains? A miracle. But as the text indicates nobody fled the prison. Prisoners willingly remaining behind bars. A second miracle!

And why did the jailer ask that specific question of Paul – *"What must I do to be saved?"* He had heard them singing praise songs all night in their cells despite being severely injured from a flogging the jailer might have administered himself.

What a testimony! God can use our faith experiences to lead others to Christ.

Psalm 127: 3

3 Sons are indeed a heritage from the LORD, offspring, a reward.
4 Like arrows in the hand of a warrior are the sons born in one's youth.

Well, I am thrilled with a granddaughter too, even though I often forget her middle name, Saide! This verse has played itself out again and again in my life.

Jason, John, Jared, Tahlon, Ben, Declan, Asa .. finally Rilynn. And still another yet to be added to our family tree! That's an amazing quiver of blessing. And I like the phrase, "heritage from the Lord". It connotes both a gift but also a future.

I remember my grandfather often saying in the latter years of his life, "I just want to find out how it all works out for you." A family enables us to engage with the future and hope for what is to come. I loved my grandad dearly. He died before I trusted Christ and had the spiritual change in life. He never met Gwen, never heard me preach, never experienced all the amazing things that have filled the subsequent chapters of this family story – his family story.

We are his heritage, the offspring of Chester Ellsworth Smart and Mary Alice Walker Smart.

Arrows in his quiver. What a blessing to know the arrows have filled another generation, that of Robert L and Mary Louise Matthews. And now a third, Gregory Robert and Gwen Speeler Matthews.

As I reach the final decades of life, these are the things I most value. Nothing compares to my children and grandchildren. Not possessions. Not work. Not experiences. I now understand that desire of my grandfather to know how it turns out for all of you. And my prayer, like his, is that it turns out to the glory of God.

Summer at EvenRidge, 2019

Esther 4:13

13 Mordecai told the messenger to reply to Esther, "Don't think that you will escape the fate of all the Jews because you are in the king's palace.
14 "If you keep silent at this time, relief and deliverance will come to the Jewish people from another place, but you and your father's family will be destroyed. Who knows, perhaps you have come to your royal position for such a time as this."

"For such a time as this", one of the great challenges of the Bible. In this book we learn about the role a young woman played in delivering her people from annihilation. Esther was made the queen of Persia at the time of a plot to destroy all Jews living in the kingdom. God had positioned her in this key role so He could bring about a miraculous deliverance. Jews around the world still celebrate this event in the feast of Purim.

God is always at work to bring deliverance and comfort. The Apostle Paul tells us He is the God of all comfort. And God often uses human instrumentality to accomplish His purpose. I ought to be looking for "such times as this" in my family, in my work, in my church, in my neighborhood. Such things become the stories we will be telling in years and decades to come.

As I reflect on that, it seems our birthday honors are a type of "Purim" where we recount the amazing grace and deliverance of God working in our midst. Look for the ways God wants to use you today and this week to pour His grace out on those around you.

Acts 20:21

"I testified to both Jews and Greeks about repentance toward God and faith in our Lord Jesus."

Studies show that fewer than 10% of Christians actively share their faith in Christ. I have to admit that I am largely part of that 90% even though I work for one of the greatest evangelism ministries in the world! This verse in Acts can help me in this necessary part of being a true follower of Jesus Christ. First, Paul says he shared with both Jews and Greeks. That is everybody, regardless of culture, race, gender, age. The gospel has a universal appeal because Jesus died for the sins of the world. Secondly, sin makes us uncomfortable because we know there is a better way to live and we aren't taking it. Admitting our wrongs and turning from them is what repentance toward God means. This, too, is universal. Finally, faith in Christ is God's only remedy for sin. Jesus bore our sin in his own body on the cross so that we can repent from it and live for God in a righteous way. That is the gospel message. Simple, yet profound. As God opens the doors to people in our lives, let's be ready to share this wonderful and applicable Good News with them.

Acts 26: 14

"Saul, Saul, why are you persecuting me? It is hard for you to kick against the goads."

What does this phrase "kicking against the goads" mean? Did a little research .. an oxgoad is the spear-like tool ranchers used to move cattle. They gently tap the hindquarters of an ox to get it moving in the right direction.

God uses goads in our lives for the same purpose. It might be a sermon, a bible text, wise counsel from a spouse or friend, even sickness or other setbacks. Their purpose is to get us to change direction.

Back to the goad: when an ox kicks against the goad, the tip of the tool embeds deeper into its skin. It hurts! Jesus was telling Saul in that road to Damascus encounter that if he (Saul) would stop resisting he would experience less pain. How often the same with us! Jesus is the Lord. He has every right and authority to guide my life. But sometimes I don't want to go in His direction. I kick against His gentle, prodding Spirit, the oxgoad of my life. How much better to simply yield to His will and let Him guide me.

Revelation 9:20-21

20 The rest of the people, who were not killed by these plagues, did not repent
of the works of their hands to stop worshiping demons and idols of gold,
silver, bronze, stone, and wood, which cannot see, hear, or walk.
21 And they did not repent of their murders, their sorceries, their sexual immorality, or their thefts.

The Apostle John describes these endtimes judgments that are coming on this earth and its godless inhabitants. It is instructive in these two verses to see an important link: bad theology leads to bad behavior. That is why Christians make a practice of attending worship regularly. At church, we encounter the person of God and His Christ. We are reminded of His great love and redemptive plan of salvation. Our minds and hearts are drawn back to biblical truth. Absent of that, a Christian easily slips back into behavior we have been redeemed from. The connection in this 9th chapter of Revelation couldn't be more clear. Prepare your family and your hearts to worship the Lord on His day tomorrow. It is the best antidote to sin.

Psalm 131:1-2

1 LORD, my heart is not proud; my eyes are not haughty. I do not get
involved with things too great or too wondrous for me.

*2 Instead, I have calmed and quieted my soul like a weaned child
with its mother; my soul is like a weaned child.*

There is a tendency in our day to engage with and then become expert in everything. It is the access to a little that leads to desire for much. That seems to lessen my focus on family, work, neighbors and church. That wider circle begins to get my attention (see Facebook!). Better to focus narrowly on those closest to me. Becoming an expert on their situations is a formula for success and contentment.

Bonus verse from **Psalm 133:1** *How good and pleasant it is when brothers live together in harmony!*

I will let each of us meditate on the tremendous truth contained in these 12 short words. And in the blessing that living this out can bring to our lives, our families, our churches, our communities, our jobs. As Saint Francis challenged us to be that "instrument of peace".

Isaiah 3:5

*"The people will oppress one another, man against man, neighbor against neighbor; the
young will act arrogantly toward the old, and the worthless toward the honorable."*

This is a nation in disarray. It was Israel during various times and under various kings. A culture turned on its head. A nation in need of serious reform. It is incumbent on Christian families to be the salt and the light of a nation and culture. Without the quiet witness of godly parents raising their children in the fear and counsel of the Lord, the message of godliness will be suppressed, even lost. Society will decay. A nation will falter.

Today we pray for our extended family .. for unsaved relatives, for others who have wandered from the faith. Let's remember to persevere in prayer for family members who need the touch of divine grace in their lives. That is crucial for our families and for our nation.

Isaiah 7:14-15 / Matthew 1:23-25

Isaiah 7:14 *"Therefore, the Lord himself will give you a sign: See, the*
virgin will conceive a son, and name him Immanuel.
15 *"By the time he learns to reject what is bad and choose what is good, he will be eating curds and honey.*

Matthew1:23 *See, the virgin will become pregnant and give birth to a son, and*
they will name him Immanuel, which is translated "God is with us."
24 *When Joseph woke up, he did as the Lord's angel had commanded him. He married her*
25 *but did not have sexual relations with her until she gave birth to a son. And he named him Jesus.*

Thursday the reading was from Isaiah. Today from Matthew. What a joy to encounter this prophecy and it's fulfillment in the same devotion. Biblical prophecy and its fulfillment is one of the great evidences about the truth of Christianity. And this is not merely our truth, it is Truth.

One sidelight of this passage is the brief discussion of what is called the age of consent or responsibility. When a child knows right from wrong, something changes. That is when the Gospel becomes their greatest need. They now own the responsibility for their sin. Be sure to pray for the salvation of our precious little ones as they approach this age of accountability: Ben, Declan, Asa and Rilynn. And thank Jesus for Tahlon's salvation on Easter, 2016.

Acts 17: 7

"and Jason has welcomed them. They are all acting contrary to Caesar's
decrees, saying that there is another king, Jesus."

I didn't realize it at the time - way back in 1974 - but we named our first born after one of the early heroes of the Faith. This Jason stood against dangerous persecution coming against the early church. Jason had responded to the Apostle Paul's gospel message, "This Jesus I am proclaiming to you is the Messiah." Jason bore immediate fruit for the gospel in his life:

5 Attacking Jason's house, they searched for them to bring them out to the public assembly.
6 When they did not find them, they dragged Jason and some of the brothers before the city officials, shouting, "These men who have turned the world upside down have come here too,
7 "and Jason has welcomed them.

He was a courageous man who refused to be intimidated, but stood with Paul and Silas, the missionaries who had preached to him. And Jason's faith was a costly one. He readily opened his resources to others.

9 "After taking a security bond from Jason and the others, they released them."

We named our Jason after the mythical Argonaut warrior. But I like this Jason better .. a good namesake for Jason Speeler Matthews.

Genesis 2:7

Here is a Bible puzzler for you to consider if you want:

7 Then the LORD God formed the man out of the dust from the ground and breathed the breath of life into his nostrils, and the man became a living being.
8 The LORD God planted a garden in Eden, in the east, and there he placed the man he had formed.
9 The LORD God caused to grow out of the ground every tree pleasing in appearance and good for food, including the tree of life in the middle of the garden, as well as the tree of the knowledge of good and evil.

In this second chapter, the creation of man seems to precede the creation of plant life. But in Genesis 1, plants are third day activity, man on the sixth. How would you reconcile this apparent contradiction?

A texting convo ensued between the Matthews guys that demonstrates how the Word challenges our thinking.

Jared: The second chapter is describing a specific place, the garden. The first chapter describes creation as a whole. So the second chapter doesn't necessarily describe the creation of man and plants in a linear sequence like the first chapter. There's no "and then" in between verse seven and eight.

Greg: Good catch. Another insight comes from the original language for the word "formed". The original has it in the pluperfect tense rather than past tense. Instead of "formed" the better translation would be "had formed". Choosing good bible translations is important!

Jason: It's also possible genesis 1-3 are completely allegorical in their description of the creation and fall of man, and each chapter might have their own particular function in the narrative which cause them to not necessarily flow linearly. If literal description of events was never the intention, I'm not sure a linear contradiction is something that necessarily compromises the truths.

John: I guess the problem with that idea is where does allegory stop and historical interpretation begin in Genesis?

Jason, John, Jared, Greg (and Asa)

Joshua 1:8

*"This book of instruction must not depart from your mouth; you are to meditate
on it day and night so that you may carefully observe everything written in
it. For then you will prosper and succeed in whatever you do."*

A succinct description of the purpose of Scripture. May this wonderful testament to divine grace and instruction be our constant guide in the Matthews clan, as illustrated by the previous discussion.

Job 1:5

Whenever a round of banqueting was over, Job would send for his children and purify them, rising early in the morning to offer burnt offerings for all of them. For Job thought, "Perhaps my children have sinned, having cursed God in their hearts."

I find this interesting. Job was not worried about the feasting where there was no doubt a measure of alcohol consumed. It was that any of them might turn away from the Lord. Partying can be a conduit for failing to follow Christ. But it is the latter that concerned Job. This teaches a good lesson. I should keep my focus on the main thing and not the sidebar issue. The main thing is always our relationship with God.

Isaiah 10:1

1 Woe to those enacting crooked statutes and writing oppressive laws
2 to keep the poor from getting a fair trial and to deprive the needy among my people
of justice, so that widows can be their spoil and they can plunder the fatherless.

God is a social justice warrior too. His concern is for the weakest and those without an advocate. Widows and orphans are His focus throughout scripture. Devising a righteous safety net should begin with these two groups of people. And, of course, defending the weakest and most vulnerable, the unborn.

Baby Girl Rilynn, 2 months

Matthew 5:3-12

3 *"Blessed are the poor in spirit, for the kingdom of heaven is theirs.*
4 *"Blessed are those who mourn, for they will be comforted.*
5 *"Blessed are the humble, for they will inherit the earth.*
6 *"Blessed are those who hunger and thirst for righteousness, for they will be filled.*
7 *"Blessed are the merciful, for they will be shown mercy. 8 "Blessed*
are the pure in heart, for they will see God.
9 *"Blessed are the peacemakers, for they will be called sons of God.*
10 *"Blessed are those who are persecuted because of righteousness, for the kingdom of heaven is theirs.*
11 *"You are blessed when they insult you and persecute you and*
falsely say every kind of evil against you because of me.
12 *"Be glad and rejoice, because your reward is great in heaven. For that*
is how they persecuted the prophets who were before you.

Commentary unnecessary in this greatest of all sermons ever delivered.

Romans 3:23

23 *For all have sinned and fall short of the glory of God.*
24 *They are justified freely by his grace through the redemption that is in Christ Jesus.*

Here is the bad news and the good news summed up in two brief verses (amazing how Scripture can get to the point with an economy of words). The Bad. All have sinned and stand guilty before a Holy God. There is no avoiding this reality and its eternal consequences.

Praise be to God the story doesn't end there. For God has established a way to deal with our fallen state. That way is the gospel of grace where you and I can be justified and redeemed through faith in

Jesus Christ. What good news! What a great story to tell our children and those we love. And how crucial to live out this grace daily as a witness to unsaved people.

Proverbs 16:7

"When a person's ways please the LORD, he makes even his enemies to be at peace with him."

The way to teach children how to make and maintain friends. Make sure what we do and say is pleasing to God. The friends will naturally follow.

Psalm 5:3-8

3 In the morning, LORD, you hear my voice; in the morning I
plead my case to you and watch expectantly.
4 For you are not a God who delights in wickedness; evil cannot dwell with you.
5 The boastful cannot stand in your sight; you hate all evildoers.
6 You destroy those who tell lies; the LORD abhors violent and treacherous people.
7 But I enter your house by the abundance of your faithful love; I bow
down toward your holy temple in reverential awe of you.
8 LORD, lead me in your righteousness because of my adversaries; make your way straight before me.

I prefer to read the Bible and have a devotional from it in the morning. (As you know well!) This Psalm outlines a morning devotional that is helpful to me. The writer approaches the Lord in the morning with a heart of repentance. He lays before God any wickedness, arrogance or lies in his life. Dealing with sin, the barrier between me and God is the first step of a devotional in Scripture. It renews my relationship with the One who is holy.

Then, comes worship (verse 7). The Bible brings me into an encounter with the Living God. That ought to elicit worship, deep respect and even awe. It is God's faithful love (what a contrast to my own fickle love) that brings me to worship who He is and how He relates to me.

Finally, a moment of re-dedication and consecration to Him (verse 8). I start the day renewed in my faith and my calling to be a witness of His grace and truth. That should start in my home and spread out to my workplace and beyond. These few moments every morning can set the heart, the mind and the spirit on a right path.

Genesis 6:5

"When the LORD saw that human wickedness was widespread on the earth and that every inclination of the human mind was nothing but evil all the time."

We know how that story ended, the Great Flood and the rescue of the human race through Noah. But that description of mankind in those days as "nothing but evil all the time" jumped out at me. We live in an age of increasing evil. Not sure it is all the time yet and thankful for that. A day is coming (when the Holy Spirit is removed) that unprecedented evil will describe human society and culture. We used to sing a hymn called "Take time to be holy". That is the great antidote to rampaging evil around us. Take some time to pray today. Take time to speak a word of encouragement to your spouse, to your children, to your neighbor or work associate. Tell somebody about your faith in God and His Christ. Be thankful for everything God has done for you. Take a little time to be holy. We can be the antidote to evil by living righteous lives like Noah.

Job 4:3-4

3 Indeed, you have instructed many and have strengthened weak hands.
4 Your words have steadied the one who was stumbling and braced the knees that were buckling.

Many things have been written about Job, the man who suffered total loss. He was a righteous man. He was steadfast in his faith despite incredible setbacks. He is an example of perseverance under the most difficult, even disastrous circumstances. But Job was also an effective mentor of others. In fact, the men who came to encourage (and accuse!) him were probably his disciples.

Job's style of teaching struck me this morning as I read these verses. He is a good pattern to follow as we instruct others. Here is a man who uses teaching and instruction to encourage, build up and fortify. That should be the way we instruct our children. Become a student of your children's strengths and weaknesses. Amplify the areas of strength. Correct the weaknesses. It would be good to focus on both so that the children aren't always hearing negative reinforcement but also have the balance of acknowledging the grace and gifting in their lives.

(Sermon from papa now ends)

23 I wish that my words were written down, that they were recorded on a scroll
24 or were inscribed in stone forever by an iron stylus and lead!
25 But I know that my Redeemer lives, and at the end he will stand on the dust.
26 Even after my skin has been destroyed, yet I will see God in my flesh.

This section of Job's lament is very interesting. He is crying out in his pain to friends who are accusing him of misdeeds he did not commit. And in his defense he makes this plaintive cry that he wishes his words would be preserved for posterity. Indeed they have been preserved and we read them today more than 3000 years later.

And his thoughts have been written into some of the most beautiful music ever produced. Verses 25-26 is the text for that well known oratorio in Handel's *Messiah*. Trapped by the moment in a difficult situation; the prison of grief. Getting the longer view is often what we need and in this glorious moment, Job looks forward to the resurrection from the dead and finds hope. In fact, you could find two resurrections in that amazing 25th verse: Job's and Jesus'. Look again ! And the next verse too.

27 "I will see him myself; my eyes will look at him, and not as a stranger. My heart longs within me."

"I will sing to the LORD because He has treated me generously."

Consider for a moment the character quality of generosity. It marks a person of high esteem. Generous people have right priorities: people before things. They set their focus on others' needs instead of their own wants. Everybody loves generous people, especially at birthday and Christmas!

Greedy, miserly are the antonyms of generosity. Not such good word pictures. My father was a generous man. He taught me that money was not an end in itself, but a means to providing for the needs of his wife, his children and his church. He once provided our family with a new car when we were on the mission field in Chicago. It was a great blessing. That's the kind of man I strive to become; using my blessings to bless others.

Mom and Dad, 2009

Amos 4:13

"He is here: the one who forms the mountains, creates the wind, and reveals his thoughts to man, the one who makes the dawn out of darkness and strides on the heights of the earth. The LORD, the God of Armies, is his name."

A wonderful and awesome description of God, the Lord of Hosts. He is the Creator of heaven and earth. He formed it all with a word from His mouth. Speaking everything into existence from nothing - ex nihilo - is what modern man objects to. We error by limiting God to our processes. With us there must be a mechanism. But God can speak His mind and things are. Amazing!

And this matter of creating the wind .. what is this but establishing all the systems of our world that sustain it. Wind is one of those systems, along with evaporation, planetary rotation, etc. The list is endless. This world is a perfect blend of ecosystems that work to sustain human life, the ultimate purpose.

Had God done only that it should have been enough to elicit our worship and highest praise. But the verse gives us yet another source for wonder in our God. He has revealed His thoughts to us. He is a transparent God. He instructs, corrects, counsels, sustains. The entire purpose of this prophet's revelation message to Israel and us.

And God has done this last piece by giving us His Word. And His Spirit. What a blessing! What a benefit to enter daily into His courts of wisdom and praise and find our God's thoughts.

I hope these little devotions adequately reveal just a little of that to all of you. His thoughts, Scripture says, are not our thoughts. But He graciously reveals Himself to us that we might trust in Him and praise His Name.

2 Peter 1:8

"For if you possess these qualities in increasing measure, they will keep you from being useless or unfruitful in the knowledge of our Lord Jesus Christ."

Equipped and deployed. That is the military and business model for accomplishing its mission. And it is what this verse invites me to consider about the Christian life too: being useful and fruitful for Christ.

Being equipped is a basic principle in any enterprise. I need to have the tools to accomplish a purpose. I think of John over in Afghanistan as part of the security team for our nation's military and diplomatic installations. His organization spends time training and equipping its security personnel to do their jobs. If they sent me over there, chaos would ensue. I am not prepared to engage a hostile force and defend an encampment.

But John has those skills. He has both the temperament and ability to engage and defend. In the Christian life, the Holy Spirit does a similar work in our lives. He cleans us up morally and prepares us spiritually to engage our enemy on the battlefield for the hearts and souls of people. He does that through the amazing gifts of the Spirit with which He sends me out.

That starts in our homes. It is our first deployment. It is what the "fruitful" element of this verse refers to. What would be the point of John's company putting him through all their extensive training only to place him somewhere in Rowan county guarding a traffic stop? He is a frontline warrior, trained for conflict and for defense.

God wants to deploy us in the battle for souls. He wants us to engage our enemy with the tools he has provided to both defend and expand His kingdom. The question I must ask daily is, "will I accept the assignment? Will I go on deployment for His kingdom?"

2 Chronicles 7:21-22

21 As for this temple, which was exalted, everyone who passes by will be appalled and will say: Why did the LORD do this to this land and this temple? 22 Then they will say: Because they abandoned the LORD God of their ancestors who brought them out of the land of Egypt. They clung to other gods and bowed in worship to them and served them. Because of this, he brought all this ruin on them.

All that remains of that great temple of Solomon are the tremendous foundation stones that the Babylonians chose not to remove when they destroyed it in 586 BC. It is now the location of the Wailing Wall where Jews from around the world go to pray. I have been there, watching as the faithful press their prayer requests on scraps of paper into the cracks between the stones. It is reminder of how God responds to idolatry - He will not abide it. First command: You shall have no other gods before me.

We live in an age when idolatry is rare in the West. Go to India or Asia and idols are common. Not here, at least, not as carved or cast objects. Our idols are different. Scripture calls materialism - the pursuit of things - a form of idolatry. We might add fame to the list, a common idol in our age.

And there are idols of the mind like intellectual pursuit, pornography, vanity (the idol of the narcissist).

Clinging to things or ideas that separate me from devotion and trust in God alone is an idol, a false god to be rejected if I want relationship with the true, living God. Let's clear away our idols and give Him sole possession of our lives. Let's remove the idols and worship Him alone in spirit and truth.

Jeremiah 16: 12

"You did more evil than your fathers. Look, each one of you was following the stubbornness of his evil heart, not obeying me."

Stubborn is being resistant to change. It is being set in my way. It is refusing to yield to God or others. It is also a Matthews characteristic. I see it in myself. I see it in my grandchildren and sons. We are a stubborn bunch.

Being stubborn can have pluses and minuses. If I am stubborn in doing what is right and good, it has a positive quality. That we might call patterned living .. finding things that work to our and others benefit.

But being stubborn in my own wants and needs before considering those of others around me is the stubbornness Jeremiah refers to. It is setting patterns that look first and foremost to ME.

The ultimate stubbornness is that towards God. It is what this prophet warns his people against. Is my pattern to avoid the pangs of conscience God might be speaking to me? Is His Word active and powerful in my life? Or am I stubbornly ignoring all the warning signs He gives me about areas He wants to change in me?

Being more pliable toward Him will yield a similar attitude toward others around me. In the coming year, I want to cultivate this yielding in my life and see the Matthews stubborn trait melting away.

Psalm 127:1

"Unless the LORD builds a house, its builders labor over it in vain; unless the LORD watches over a city, the watchman stays alert in vain."

I am building my first house as the contractor. In that role, I must find a plan, gather resources, contract with subs, coordinate activities, set deadlines, pay for work completed, complete inspections. It is a daunting task.

I haven't cut a single board or nailed them together. Others do that. My role is to oversee the operation. To coordinate. Sometimes to urge when others fail to act in a timely way. To keep the project on schedule.

That is what I think this verse is telling us about how God works in our lives. He is an overseer. He is primarily responsible for the big picture. He manages the various stages and tasks that comprise a life-change.

I am grateful He is a master builder. Just look at the awesome world he made for us. The perfection of the cosmos should encourage me to allow God to build the foundations and edifice of my life. He is a proven architect of beauty and function. Let Him construct your life in this same way.

Acts 9: 1

*1 Now Saul was still breathing threats and murder against the
disciples of the Lord. He went to the high priest
2 and requested letters from him to the synagogues in Damascus, so that if he found any men
or women who belonged to the <u>Way</u>, he might bring them as prisoners to Jerusalem.*

It is interesting to me how Luke, the church's first historian refers to the early Church. After writing the Gospel account of Jesus' birth, ministry, death and resurrection, Luke continues his narrative. In the account of the Acts of the Apostles, we learn how the Gospel of Christ spread around the Roman world. And here in this 9th chapter this new spiritual movement is given (or has adopted) its branding. "The Way".

I work with churches. In the past 19 years I have been in thousands of churches. None were called by this early Christian moniker. There are Baptists, Lutherans, Methodists, Anglicans, Presbyterians. And many, many more. I googled the name The Way. There are a few individual congregations scattered about the country. Just a handful. Yet, this was how that early church or the culture it grew up in labeled the new spiritual movement of God.

The Way. *"I am the way, the truth and the life."* (John 14:6) *"Trust in the Lord .. He will direct your Ways."* (Proverbs 3:5-6).

It's a good name to live under. It tells me God has a purpose for me. In Christ, I can follow a certain path of righteousness that leads to abundant and eternal life.

The Way is narrow. But it is smooth and without stumbling stones. It is paved with promises that make it easy and light to traverse. Not always, but generally and finally. I like that name, The Way. In a world where people and society has lost its bearings, it stands as a signpost to the lost. Follow Jesus. He will show you the way

Psalm 125:2

"The mountains surround Jerusalem and the LORD surrounds his people, both now and forever."

We are literally surrounded by mountains here in Maggie Valley. (See cover photo.) Plott Balsam (6020 feet). Waterrock and Browning Knobs (both exceeding 6200 feet). What a wonderful word picture of being completely encompassed about by our God who is a tower of strength to us.

Psalm 121:1-2

1 I lift my eyes toward the mountains. Where will my help come from?
2 My help comes from the LORD, the Maker of heaven and earth.

Here is another wonderful mountain picture from Scripture that is so well illustrated by our present location in the Great Smokies. The One who made these majestic heights is the One who lends His help to me.

James 1:3

"... because you know that the testing of your faith produces endurance."

Trials in life must be avoided at all costs in the culture that seeks pleasure and avoids pain at all cost. Our culture. But James is telling us that trials can actually serve a greater purpose in our lives. In fact, the path to spiritual maturity must include trials.

Christians have endured the trials of ostracism, persecution, rejection throughout the history of the church. It has strengthened the faith and caused it to endure and even flourish. But how are we, in the age of plenty to relate to this verse? Perhaps we are tempted in a different way, by the excesses of our times.

Access to everything has its tests as well. Do I live within my means? Do I save resources for the future? Do I use everything on myself or do I give to others and to God? Is my life shaped by acquisition or is it a product of my beliefs? Can I remain thankful for the many blessings bestowed on me and even be grateful for the obstacles that life presents?

Even in this age of abundance, James message can challenge us to let our unique trials finish the work God has begun in our lives.

Hosea 5:4

"Their actions do not allow them to return to their God, for a spirit of promiscuity is among them, and they do not know the LORD."

I find this verse interesting in light of our culture. The promiscuity referenced is spiritual. Israel had turned to idols in violation of the commandments God had given them. It was inhibiting them from repenting and getting right with the Lord.

There are certain sinful behaviors that so cloud our thinking we are then unable to recognize sin for what it is. And thus, our ability to break from it and return to the path of righteousness is blocked.

I have seen this in the area of promiscuity. In my years as a pastor, I encountered a number of pastoral situations where a man or woman was unfaithful in marriage. When it was exposed, seldom did that person make a clean break from their pattern. It lingered on and destroyed their relationship and their family.

This verse in Hosea is wise counsel. It directs me away from being promiscuous because the consequences are so severe .. inability to return to God and to the relationship I have ruined.

Deuteronomy 10:12

*"And now, Israel, what does the LORD your God ask of you except to fear
the LORD your God by walking in all his ways, to love him, and to worship
the LORD your God with all your heart and all your soul?"*

Three foundational principles of a relationship with God. These were given by Moses to the nation of Israel as it entered the Promised Land. And they remain true for the people of God in our age too.

A healthy respect for a holy God which produces godly living. Fear of God is not to be confused with the word "afraid". It is better understood as deepest respect. That deep respect is behavior-altering. It induces me to obey what God says about things, to "walk in His ways."

Respect alone without love makes a relationship sterile emotionally. God wants my respect. He also wants my love because He is an emotional being. Love is one of God's greatest gifts. It uniquely defines a human being from every living thing God made. I would like to think my dog loves me. But truly, she sees me as her food source. Love elevates the relationship from the functional (body) to the emotional (soul).

The fear of God and love for Him yields worship. This is spiritual. God is like us so that we can love Him. But he is also unique from us. He is transcendent. He is beyond everything we know and experience. That is our reason to worship Him.

It is a relationship of body, soul and spirit, mirrored in the marriage or even parental relationships, both of which God uses to define His relationship with us. What a blessing to realize that in our homes we have the ability to reflect this divine relationship in our daily lives with each other.

Hebrews 11:3

(This devotional is admittedly lengthy. Apologies)
*"By faith we understand that the universe was created by the word of God,
so that what is seen was made from things that are not visible."*

Here is the great clash of worldviews in our age. The materialist view that insists everything in the cosmos came from what was already here (but how did it get here?). That is in opposition to the biblical view of creation where God created the cosmos from nothing.

In fact, this verse written 2000 years ago anticipates the present Darwinian age. "What is seen was made from things that are NOT visible." Darwin's theory requires a closed system for the cosmos. All the elements are contained within our universe and always have been. Life emerged from DNA, the simplest building block and through mutation and time arrived at increasingly complex life forms.

Scripture assigns creation to a Creator. It is an open system. And the biblical account insists that He spoke things into existence. In other words, what exists came from His word and power alone, not from things that already were.

Hebrews 11 gives us a single path to engage with this biblical truth. It is not through reason, although the biblical account is not unreasonable. It is not mystical. It is also not cultural or scientific or any other way our present age attempts to grasp the cosmos. It is understood through faith. That alone unlocks the door to understanding our world and ourselves.

This chapter is a wonderful exposition of how faith in God leads us to truth about what He has done, especially as a creator and as a redeemer of our souls.

I sat in a restaurant in Jacksonville this past week listening in on a conversation between a man and a woman a table over. He was loudly proclaiming his rejection of the "Christian God" and his rather certainty that no God exists. His background had been in a strict Lutheran home, where he had attended regular Sunday services as a child with his family. But he had long since left his faith roots and set out on his own theological and moral course absent any belief in a Divine being.

As I listened to his exposition of truth, it occurred to me that I once believed like he did. I had rejected the God I was taught from youth. I had forged my own theology and morality. And it led to abject despair. So I prayed for this man and for the woman in the conversation who seemed to be a person of faith.

At that point, this fellow announced to the woman (and to most of us in the restaurant - he was loud and a little drunk) that his husband was a very smart fellow.

His husband. To be continued

Romans 1:25-27

Faith leads me into a relationship with my Creator and Redeemer according to yesterday's verse in Hebrews. Rejecting Him leads me to another place, where the man I described yesterday had arrived. The Apostle Paul explains where rejection of God can lead.

25 They exchanged the truth of God for a lie, and worshiped and served what has been created instead of the Creator, who is praised forever. Amen.
26 For this reason God delivered them over to disgraceful passions. Their women exchanged natural sexual relations for unnatural ones.
27 The men in the same way also left natural relations with women and were inflamed in their lust for one another. Men committed shameless acts with men and received in their own persons the appropriate penalty of their error.

Faith in God, our Creator/Redeemer is the answer for this gay man's situation that I encountered in the Jacksonville restaurant. Returning to the truths this man was given as a child in the Lutheran church would change his sexual orientation. That is my prayer for him and for others trapped in the same condition.

The Hebrews passage makes that last point much better than I have.

6 "Now without faith it is impossible to please God, since the one who draws near to him must believe that he exists and that he rewards those who seek him."

Acts 1:11

"They said, 'Men of Galilee, why do you stand looking up into heaven? This same Jesus, who has been taken from you into heaven, will come in the same way that you have seen him going into heaven.'

The next great event in human history will not be the re-election of a new president (Donald

Trump at the present time .. if indeed that happens). It will not be the cure for cancer, although that will also be something to celebrate. It will be when this verse is fulfilled and Christ returns.

A few years ago a group of journalists was asked what the greatest headline they could imagine would be. Most said, "Jesus returns to earth." The Second Coming of Christ lurks in the back of our minds. When or will this great event take place? Will it be in my lifetime? Am I ready for it to happen?

That last question is what grabbed my mind this morning. Am I ready? Ready spiritually? Ready morally? Ready relationally? Are my affairs in order in this life to begin the eternal life to come? And those questions seemed to all hinge on a further, more basic question .. do I desire the Second Coming of Christ, or would I rather see that blessed event delayed a little longer?

I noticed that as my mother entered her final years and her life became more and more difficult even with the loving care my sister and her family provided, her earnest desire for the rapture and return of Jesus became more and more acute. As the value and joy of living became less and less, her anticipation of the next life grew greater. What am I grasping in this present life? Seeing the Ducks win just one national championship in football? Completing our plans at the cabin we call EvenRidge? Watching a grandson or granddaughter walk the marriage aisle?

"Lord, give me the faith and vision to see a greater existence with You than even the wonderful one I have."

Psalm 78:5

5 He established a testimony in Jacob and set up a law in Israel, which
he commanded our fathers to teach to their children
6 so that a future generation —children yet to be born — might
know. They were to rise and tell their children
7 so that they might put their confidence in God and not forget God's works, but keep his commands.

Here are some excellent points in raising godly offspring. First, the primary role of teaching spiritual formation lies with parents. It should not be outsourced to the Sunday School, a Christian school or any other institution. It belongs in the home.

Secondly, children must be taught to trust in God - put their confidence in Him. When there is a family need, pray to the Lord for His provision and direction. Let children see that God answers our prayers and meets ours and others needs.

Thirdly, the family "story" our children learn should be well spiced with our encounters of faith in God and in His provisions for us.

Finally, we must actively encourage our children to not only obey us, but to obey the Lord. They should know His commands for their lives and be encouraged to follow them.

Proverbs Devotional

Some Proverbial wisdom this morning to consider:

Proverbs 28:9 *Anyone who turns his ear away from hearing the law —even his prayer is detestable.*
Proverbs 28:14 *Happy is the one who is always reverent, but one who hardens his heart falls into trouble.*
Proverbs 29:17 *Discipline your child, and it will bring you peace of mind and give you delight.*
Proverbs 30:8 *Keep falsehood and deceitful words far from me. Give*
me neither poverty nor wealth; feed me with the food I need.
9 Otherwise, I might have too much and deny you, saying, "Who is the LORD?"
or I might have nothing and steal, profaning the name of my God.

I also read through the 31ˢᵗ Proverb about the godly wife that Jason referenced while giving Stacey his birthday honor. Here is a section I find descriptive of the three women at that party .. Gwen, Brooke and Stacy.

Proverbs 32:25 *Strength and honor are her clothing, and she can laugh at the time to come.*
26 Her mouth speaks wisdom, and loving instruction is on her tongue.
27 She watches over the activities of her household and is never idle.
28 Her children rise up and call her blessed; her husband also praises her:
29 "Many women have done noble deeds, but you surpass them all!"
30 Charm is deceptive and beauty is fleeting, but a woman who fears the LORD will be praised.
31 Give her the reward of her labor, and let her works praise her at the city gates.

"Thank You Father, for the women of our family. Truly you have blessed us with their gifts, abilities and faith."

Ecclesiastes 10:2

"A wise person's heart goes to the right, but a fool's heart to the left."

I know this is taken completely out of context but I love this verse. It validates my right-wing, conservative viewpoints! I was that left-wing radical earlier in life. Then God showed me the way to eternal life in Christ and the new life He gave me from the chaos and dissipation I had created. I was that fool given a new choice to be wise.

"Thank you Jesus for showing me that You are the Truth and the Life."

Ecclesiastes 1:8

For all of his purported wisdom, I think Solomon missed some valuable things in life. Here's an example.

8 All things are wearisome, more than anyone can say. The eye is
not satisfied by seeing or the ear filled with hearing.
9 What has been is what will be, and what has been done is what
will be done; there is nothing new under the sun.

Solomon seems to be saying, "been there done that. Boring. And life is tedious." But I disagree. I never tire of the view at EvenRidge. Each new occasion brings joy and wonder. Or take the 150th (or more!) hearing of Tchaikovsky's 5th symphony which I experienced yesterday on my drive to Charlotte. It seemed as satisfying and enjoyable to me as when I first fell in love with it at 13 years of age. I agree with Solomon that adventure and discovery are a key component of joyful living. But he concludes that at some point adventure evades him for "there is nothing new under the sun." I think he missed the opportunity of re-discovery as a source of adventure.

We watched Dances with Wolves last night for the umpteenth time. It was a delight. It brought tears of wonder and joy. The same is true of our relationships. I look forward to re-discoveries with my wife of 47+ years. We cover much of the same ground in our interactions. But it brings the joy of a fresh event nonetheless. It is an ongoing adventure I can never become bored or tired of. Perhaps Solomon tried to cram too much into his life (how many wives and concubines did he have?) and in so-doing missed the greater joys and discoveries life holds ... re-tracing well-trod paths with new perceptions and reformed expectations. That is how I intend to live out my remaining years.

Hosea 2:19

*19 I will take you to be my wife forever. I will take you to be my wife
in righteousness, justice, love, and compassion.
20 I will take you to be my wife in faithfulness, and you will know the LORD.*

God used the dysfunctional marriage of the prophet Hosea to illustrate His relationship with Israel. But in the text are nuggets of what God sees as a functioning marriage and the building blocks of that successful relationship.

Here are five: righteousness - the propensity to pursue what is right and avoid what is wrong. It's a series of small choices that governs my thoughts, my speech and my actions.

Justice - whenever two people share life, there will inevitably be conflict. Justice insures that both sides are aired and considered and that mutually beneficial decisions are made. Injustice is the exercise of self-centered power that destroys relationships.

Love - a careful reading of 1 Corinthians 13:4 (often done at the wedding ceremony) would be a beneficial monthly exercise for Gwen and me. It would remind us what biblical love looks like. *"Love is patient. Love is kind ..."*

Compassion - having a broken heart over the things that break my spouse's heart, my children's hearts. Closely identifying with their suffering (too easy to ignore it or worse, blow it off).

Faithfulness - the scripture often couples the words love and faithfulness. They are nearly synonymous. I think of it as having an extremely narrow view of what is important, my wife's needs.

Five building blocks for a good marriage. Praying God's grace will add each of them to our marriages so that they will define our homes.

1 Chronicles 28:9

"As for you, Solomon my son, know the God of your father, and serve him wholeheartedly and with
a willing mind, for the LORD searches every heart and understands the intention of every thought.
If you seek him, he will be found by you, but if you abandon him he will reject you forever."

King David's charge to his son Solomon as he commissions him to carry on the work of building the temple in Jerusalem. A good pattern to follow in our families, too.

Know God. Serve God. And do so fully engaged with heart and mind. Seek Him and don't abandon Him. May it also be with each of us!

Psalm 36:9

"For the wellspring of life is with you. By means of your light we see light."

Two things that are difficult to find outside a relationship with Jesus Christ. Spiritual refreshment (He is the living water). And guidance (He is the Light of the World).

Judges 2:1

1 "I led you up from Egypt and brought you to the land of which I swore to
your fathers; and I said, 'I will never break My covenant with you.
2 'And you shall make no covenant with the inhabitants of this land; you shall tear
down their altars.' But you have not obeyed My voice. Why have you done this?
3 "Therefore I also said, 'I will not drive them out before you; but they shall
be thorns in your side, and their gods shall be a snare to you.'"

Israel's great offensive to take the land of Canaan and fulfill all of Gods promises to Abraham had stalled. The previous book of Joshua is an account of one glorious victory after another as the Promised Land was conquered and occupied by new tenants. But by the end of the first chapter in the next historical account - Judges - the conquest ended. Why? Verse 2 gives the reason. Theirs was a faith that did not produce obedience. It was a form of godliness that lacked power to overcome obstacles and opposition. Words without actions.

We face the same crossroads in our faith journey with God. Ours can be a faith that is "all show, no go". And like Israel, we then find ourselves being snared by the spiritual thorns that once brought us to faith in the first place. God has a better way: faith that continues the conquest and offers the ongoing fulfillment of His promises. Will I fight the good fight of faith today?

John 20:31

"But these are written so that you may believe that Jesus is the Messiah, the Son of God, and that by believing you may have life in his name."

The purpose of all scripture and especially the Gospels is this: God wants us to believe, to have faith in Him and all He has done. He also wants each one of us to have eternal life and a full, meaningful life on this side of eternity.

These things are the outcome of belief in the person and the redemptive work of Jesus Christ. Faith in Christ is no small matter. It is the necessary step to a life God intends for every human being. Which brings to mind another verse in Acts 16:31 – *"Believe on the Lord Jesus Christ and you will be saved."*

1 Thessalonians 2:12

"We encouraged, comforted, and implored each one of you to live worthy of God, who calls you into his own kingdom and glory."

Being overloaded with "how to" instructions can weigh a parent down. Here Paul gives us three succinct instructions for being an effective father. Encourage. Comfort. Implore to godly lives. Simple, yet so effective. Let's try it!

Proverbs 1:3

3 .. for receiving wise instruction in righteousness, justice, and integrity;
4 for teaching shrewdness to the inexperienced, knowledge and discretion to a young man —
5 a wise man will listen and increase his learning, and a discerning man will obtain guidance —

Look at all the things a careful consideration of the Proverbs can do. Feed our children a steady diet of these nuggets of biblical truth. They will gain so much from them; shrewdness, knowledge, discretion, guidance.

1 Kings 20:11

The king of Israel answered, "Say this: 'Don't let the one who puts
on his armor boast like the one who takes it off.' "

Scripture often has the most delightful sayings. This is one of them. A neighbor king had challenged Israel in this incident, making threatening statements about what he planned to do. Israel's king responded in ways similar to our own euphemisms. "Don't get too happy in the first quarter." Boasting is odious at any time. But especially when the boaster hasn't done anything. That is arrogant foolishness. Better to wait until there are real accomplishments. Then decide whether to boast or, better yet, let the actions speak for themselves. That is humility.

Numbers 32:23

"But if you don't do this, you will certainly sin against the LORD; be sure your sin will catch up with you."

One of the most useful biblical truths to instill in our children and to recall in our own lives. It is easy to deceive myself into thinking that if nobody sees my wrong doing, I will escape accountability. Hiding my sin is never a good thing to do. Because in the end, as this verse asserts, it will be discovered.

As parents, we have found out about our sons' misbehaviors years, even decades after the fact. In most of these cases, the wrongdoer has exposed his errors with a chuckle and a good story of keeping mom and dad in the dark.

Of course, we are glad the offense didn't bring a harsh consequence, whether from the law or from God Himself.

And that is Who will ultimately reveal our transgressions. Wouldn't it be better to simply confess them now and receive divine forgiveness than to face judgment on a day to come?

Proverbs 30:8

8 Give me neither poverty nor riches-- Feed me with the food allotted to me;
9 Lest I be full and deny You, And say, "Who is the LORD?" Or lest
I be poor and steal, and profane the name of my God.

Gwen and I are celebrating our anniversary this weekend.

It is a good time to reflect back on nearly a half century of experiences, highs, lows, changes, provisions, mercies and grace.

We early on adopted a favorite theme in our marriage not unlike the verse above. It was a phrase of Friedrich Nietzsche, the German philosopher who I had greatly admired in college. The phrase .. "Praised be a little poverty." It used to hang on a plaque in our homes.

I'm reflecting today on the philosophy of enough versus the philosophy of more. So many avenues to take from that comparison/contrast. One: Enough yields greater gratitude; More, unfulfilled expectations. Enough produces contentment; More, dissatisfaction. At least that is how we see it.

Have a blessed worship in the presence of a God who is more than enough.

Psalm 73:11

The wicked say, "How can God know? Does the Most High know everything?"

And the answer to this question: "Indeed He does know everything". To Him we must all give an account for our actions and even our thoughts. That fact is the great self- regulator in the Christian life. How often would I have gone off on a wild tangent had it not been for the restraining Hand and the still small Voice speaking "to me you must give an account".

Accountability is a good thing. Spouses ought to be accountable to each other. Employees should be accountable to those who give them jobs. Politicians to the voters.

But beyond the human accountable foundation is our accountability to God. And the good news is that when we fail in our commitments to Him and each other we have a wonderful principle He gave us .. confession/forgiveness.

Ecclesiastes 3:2

".. a time to give birth and a time to die"

Ecclesiastes is rich in its insights this morning and this verse impacted me greatly to the point of tears. It was slightly less than a year ago, I watched my mother take her final breath in this world. A time to die. Yet, in less than one month God-willing, another Matthews girl will take her first breath. (And looking back now as I edit this, that little one did arrive healthy and loved.)

There are times for these things. Easy to get lost in pressing conditions that we mistake for "ultimate" situations, without considering there is a God-ordained flow of life that carries from season to season.

A time for each thing to happen.

I prefer to live life not captive to each moment but rather fully experiencing each moment in a greater context of its season. And each season encompassed by the timeless will of the Father. In fact, He created each of them on the fourth day of Creation and He sustains them to this day.

Ecclesiastes 5:2

"Do not be hasty to speak, and do not be impulsive to make a speech before God.
God is in heaven and you are on earth, so let your words be few."

Here is the wisdom of few and considered words. Probably good counsel for the Matthews men, beginning with the patriarch. This is our wedding anniversary. And in those decades I have learned a key truth: Always have the last word in your home .. "Yes, dear".

A second thought from the wisdom of the old man Solomon that is very useful in maintaining relationships.

Ecclesiastes 7:8 *The end of a matter is better than its beginning;*
a patient spirit is better than a proud spirit.

Resolution of issues is the goal of good relations. And patience fosters resolution whereas pride inflames conflict and slows the resolution. How true! Ego usually gets in the way when we are in conflict situations. And the alternative is patience. Good to practice as the situation requires.

2 Samuel 7:18

"Then King David went in, sat in the LORD's presence, and said, Who am I,
Lord GOD, and what is my house that you have brought me this far?"

I have been reflecting in the same way over the past few days. That is what many years of marriage will do. God has added so richly to our lives, sons and daughters. Grandchildren. Experiences and wealth (relatively). Salvation and service to Him. I would call my life an "abundance from God". He has brought me so far over these decades with Gwen. What can I give Him but thanks and praise.

On a slightly sadder note I met with an old friend in Portland last night. He has been diagnosed with a motor neuron disease, a type of ALS. It's almost identical to what took our dear Scott Evans life. A slow-moving, debilitating disease that has virtually paralyzed him and put him in a wheel chair.

Important to realize that the end of life comes to all of us, some sooner and some later. Some more painful than others. Take the fullness and abundance God gives and turn it into praise to God and service to others.

Proverbs 21:16-17

Here is good advice to consider:

> *16 The person who strays from the way of prudence will come*
> *to rest in the assembly of the departed spirits.*
> *17 The one who loves pleasure will become poor; whoever loves wine and oil will not get rich.*

Prudence and pleasure. Living a wise life avoids pitfalls that will undo me. By contrast, seeking pleasure is not the way to tangible gain. How counter-intuitive to the American culture that measures success by the amount of pleasure I extract from life.

Proverbs 28:26

The one who trusts in himself is a fool, but one who walks in wisdom will be safe.

As I read this piece of wisdom today I was moved to deep reflection. My dear brother-in-law is with the Lord, having breathed his last just recently. It devastated me despite knowing he is with the Savior. Our lives intertwined at key moments often in the form of rescue. As a young man, my life was described by that Proverb, trusting in myself and experiencing the fool's outcome. By the time I was 30, I had burned through at least five career start-ups; academic (University of Victoria), television journalism (three times), entrepreneur (Tourvision). Twice during those "busts" my brother-in-law was there to bail our family out - once in Nome, Alaska, the other in Hilo, Hawaii. I was living the "self-made" man philosophy to my family's destruction. Scott and Denise were my safety net.

Then one night, alone in Portland as I wrestled with my broken life, God spoke to me with a simple, profound proverbial truth that has become my life verse: "Trust in the Lord with all your heart." I ceased doing life my way, the foolish way, and started trusting God to direct my path and utilize my abilities.

A few months later I had the joy of returning to Scott and Denise some of the grace and mercy they had bestowed on me and my family when they turned up on our doorstep in Portland. We housed them through a crisis and even saw God transform their marriage and family in the same way He was transforming ours.

What a wonderful year, 1981. Trusting in self is the way of the fool, as the Proverb states. But trusting in the Lord is a sure path to a righteous, productive life. I'm a living example of this truth.

Mark 8:37

"What will a man give in exchange for his soul?"

Jesus asked this most poignant question. My brother-in-law Scott Evans has the answer to that question today. He is able to weigh everything this world offered him against the riches of knowing Christ and the eternal life to come. Scott entered God's presence this week.

If there is prayer for the lost and unsaved in heaven, Scott is praying as never before that his loved ones will not make the eternal mistake of exchanging this existence, the temporal, for the eternal one: The life that he has now entered with Christ in glory. The Day of Departure fast approaches for all of us. Temporal myopia clouds our values, choices and desires. We are not a people for this time and place. Our existence is eternal and Christ-centered. Let's renew our faith and live for Christ and the eternal life He is preparing for us.

Philippians 3:20 *"But our citizenship is in heaven, and we eagerly wait for a Savior from there, the Lord Jesus Christ. 21 He will transform the body of our humble condition into the likeness of his glorious body, by the power that enables him to subject everything to himself.*

Judges 6: 1-2

1 The Israelites did what was evil in the sight of the LORD. So the
LORD handed them over to Midian seven years,
2 and they oppressed Israel. Because of Midian, the Israelites made hiding
places for themselves in the mountains, caves, and strongholds.

Good to have EvenRidge, our mountain retreat in the Great Smokies of Western North Carolina if what happened in Israel during the time of Judges ever happens here in America. The very thought of a national calamity so great as to force our family into forest hiding is almost unthinkable. But it made me consider the great benefit of living in this Age of Grace because of what Jesus accomplished on the cross. For sure, we will reap what we sow as Galatians points out. But having the type of severe judgment from God on sin is not how it seems to work in our day as compared to the age of Judges in the Old Testament.

Praise Him for Divine mercy and grace we have received because of what Jesus did on the cross to bear our sins and limit the judgment we rightly deserve.

Proverbs 9: 10

"The fear of the LORD is the beginning of wisdom, and the knowledge of the Holy One is understanding."

It is important to note in this most prescient verse that at their core, a wise person has correct theology. That is Solomon's argument. Attending the right university can build on wisdom. It can add to the foundation. But the cornerstone of being wise is a right attitude toward God.

No wonder that the great universities of our land began as seminaries to train the pastors of our communities. And that right relationship to God is here defined as "the fear of the Lord". Fear is a deep respect for His Person and His works. It is a core acknowledgment that He made and sustains all things. It is immersing myself in His redemptive work in my life and yielding to the call of His Word. By casting off the fear of the Lord, we become fools and bear the consequence of foolishness.

It was interesting to me that Vice President Pence is calling for Americans to return to this fear of the Lord in the wake of these mass shootings in El Paso, TX and Dayton, OH. Our nation is in a spiritual crisis. And our way forward, both collectively and individually is a healthy relationship with God, and a fear of the Almighty.

Job 10:22

Something very serious to consider from the account of Job on a Godless afterlife.

"It is a land of blackness like the deepest darkness, gloomy and chaotic, where even the light is like the darkness."

Beloved, make your eternity certain now.

"The one who believes in the Son has eternal life."
(John 3:36)

Jeremiah 10:10, 12

Six great attributes of our God to meditate on before sleep tonight. Find them and worship.

"But the LORD is the true God; he is the living God and eternal King. The earth quakes at his wrath, and the nations cannot endure his rage. 12 He made the earth by his power, established the world by his wisdom, and spread out the heavens by his understanding."

Psalm 8:1-9

1 Lord, our Lord, how magnificent is your name throughout the earth! You have covered the heavens with your majesty.

2 From the mouths of infants and nursing babies, you have established a stronghold
on account of your adversaries in order to silence the enemy and the avenger.
3 When I observe your heavens, the work of your fingers, the moon and the stars, which you set in place,
4 what is a human being that you remember him, a son of man that you look after him?
5 You made him little less than God and crowned him with glory and honor.
6 You made him ruler over the works of your hands; you put everything under his feet:
7 all the sheep and oxen, as well as the animals in the wild,
8 the birds of the sky, and the fish of the sea that pass through the currents of the seas.
9 LORD, our Lord, how magnificent is your name throughout the earth!

I remember teaching Jason's 5th grade Sunday school class at Laurel Park Bible. And we made this psalm into a music video. The one scene I remember was a shot of one of the students swinging high in the Park then jumping out of the swing. I wonder now where we thought that fit. Fond memories of that class. Where are they all today in their walk of faith? "Lord, hold them tight in Your hand."

Matthew 8:13

"Then Jesus told the centurion, 'Go. As you have believed, let it be done
for you.' And his servant was healed that very moment."

Here is a moment in Jesus' ministry when He pulls back the curtain on divine action for this Roman soldier and for us. Faith is the key element to see God at work in my life. Do I lack something in Christ? Ask and believe.

Matthew 11:28-30

28 "Come to me, all of you who are weary and burdened, and I will give you rest.
29 "Take up my yoke and learn from me, because I am lowly and
humble in heart, and you will find rest for your souls.
30 "For my yoke is easy and my burden is light."

One of my favorite passages. Who doesn't desire that kind of deep, inner rest that Christ promises his yoke-fellows. It's not a burden to follow Jesus. It's not a drag. When I am in step with Him, there should be rest, ease and lightened burden. Sometimes I think we make it too difficult because we're doing our own thing and not working in tandem with the Savior.

Proverbs 15:1

"A gentle answer turns away anger, but a harsh word stirs up wrath."

In my first few years of being a new Christian, I met with a group of men who learned verses from the Proverbs. They were called tongue-tamers, Scripture that prompted us to gain mastery over our words. This was one of those verses.

We would be wise to teach our children this proverb. In the heat of conflict, Solomon reminds us how to cool and diffuse a hostile situation. I have seen how this often works in our texting debates. Instead of firing back, someone will use quiet reason and hostility is averted. Let's practice this wisdom and demonstrate it in our homes so the next generation can use their tongues for healing.

Psalm 18:30

30 God - his way is perfect; the word of the LORD is pure. He is a shield to all who take refuge in him. 31 For who is God besides the LORD? And who is a rock? Only our God.

Five things to know about the Lord God from these two short verses. He is perfect, pure, a shield and refuge, and He is a rock. What more can I need but the Lord God Almighty.

Genesis 28:20

20 Then Jacob made a vow: "If God will be with me and watch over me during this journey I'm making, if he provides me with food to eat and clothing to wear,
21 "and if I return safely to my father's family, then the LORD will be my God.
22 "This stone that I have set up as a marker will be God's house, and I will give to you a tenth of all that you give me."

Here is the second example (Abraham being the first) of people responding to God's grace with the tithe. This is before the tithe was commanded of Israel in the Mosaic Law. It shows that our natural response to God's kindness is to give back to Him.

Are we giving to God in proportion to the benefits we have received from Him? Is our giving regular, proportional and done with joy .. the New Testament measures of giving?

Matthew 5:24

Great teaching from the Sermon on the Mount this morning at a church in Kennewick, WA where I was working on a Decision Northwest project for BGEA. The pastor nailed this passage for his congregation.

"Leave your gift there in front of the altar. First go and be reconciled with your brother or sister"

Here were the five principles he gave for reconciliation when relationships are broken:

1. You go. This is the responsibility of the one who is aware of the problem.
2. You go now. Don't wait and stew. I should be compelled to get this taken care of. Another passage talks about not letting the sun go down on anger.
3. You go alone. In his passage on conflict resolution, Jesus says the first encounter should be one-on-one.

4. You go to reconcile. Keep the thing, the thing. Don't get distracted onto other business. Settle the matter at hand.

5. Finally, let go .. of your right to punish or hold onto the offense.

Another great principle: Offense is an event; offended is a choice. We can't always choose the events that cause offense. But we can choose to live in that offense. Forgiveness is the way out of living offended lives.

Jeremiah 31:33

"Instead, this is the covenant I will make with the house of Israel after those days" - the LORD's declaration. 'I will put my teaching within them and write it on their hearts. I will be their God, and they will be my people.'"

This wonderful promise has been literally fulfilled in the church. Every believer has the Holy Spirit living inside them. And He puts on our hearts everything God desires for His people. Being sensitive and obedient to the leading of the Spirit is our task as Christians. May He have His way in our lives, even this day.

1 Peter 3:10-12

A word about the proactive Christian life:

10 For the one who wants to love life and to see good days, let him keep his tongue from evil and his lips from speaking deceit,
11 and let him turn away from evil and do what is good. Let him seek peace and pursue it,
12 because the eyes of the Lord are on the righteous and his ears are open to their prayer. But the face of the Lord is against those who do what is evil.

Hosea 10:12

"Sow righteousness for yourselves and reap faithful love; break up your unplowed ground. It is time to seek the LORD until he comes and sends righteousness on you like the rain."

This promise was given to Israel in the middle of a prophecy about judgment. The prophet railed against the evils in Israel and how God was about to punish their lawlessness. But I like the fact that God always gives His people the path to repentance and blessing if we will take it.

A second thought this morning from **Hosea 14:2**

Take words of repentance with you and return to the LORD. Say to him: "Forgive all our iniquity and accept what is good, so that we may repay you with praise from our lips."

Salvation is a free gift of God. I can do nothing to earn it. But this verse is interesting. Though salvation is free I can repay God for that gracious gift by giving Him praise. May the Name be praised in our family this day.

"O Jesus, how wonderful You are. What an amazing Savior!"

Mark 3:25

"If a house is divided against itself, that house cannot stand."

A short thought to guide our home life. It is so important for a family to be of one accord. United in faith. United in love. One in purpose. Shared goals and visions. Building a common history. As these things coalesce, a family can be strong and enduring.

What are the ways I contribute to the unity of my family?

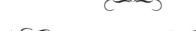

1 Corinthians 1:23-25

Here is the message that will never be dated, obsolete or passé.

23 But we preach Christ crucified, a stumbling block to the Jews and foolishness to the Gentiles.
24 Yet to those who are called, both Jews and Greeks, Christ is the power of God and the wisdom of God,
25 because God's foolishness is wiser than human wisdom, and
God's weakness is stronger than human strength.

May the cross of Jesus Christ be the first thought and word on our minds and tongues this day. Let the children know that God loves them.

Exodus 2:25

"And God saw the Israelites; and God knew."

This is the time when the Israelites were being oppressed by the Egyptians. And their God-ordained deliverer Moses had fled to Midian after killing the Egyptian. The human condition was bleak. But God's eye had never left the people He had promised through Abraham and Isaac. He saw their condition. He saw them.

And the text also says "He knew". What did God know? His century old covenant with their ancestor Abraham? His plan to deliver Israel from its circumstances? His fulfillment of that Abrahamic promise in the land of Canaan? The heart of this people to backslide? The text doesn't say, but we could surmise all of the above.

It's good to know that God's faithfulness to His promises are not dependent on our performance. If that were the case, we would still be under law .. and doomed to failure. Rather, His promises and mercy and grace are new every morning. Great is His faithfulness. (Lamentations 3:23)

"Thank you, Father, for looking on our circumstances and knowing best how to deal with them. We trust in You for our needs this day."

Job 38:2

"Who is this who obscures my counsel with ignorant words."

After a long and intense discussion between Job and his "friends" over the nature of sin, righteousness and judgment, God weighs in for the first time. This book of the Old Testament is an interesting examination of that old conundrum, "Why do bad things happen to good people?"

Both Job and his friends have reached wrong conclusions: the friends about the reason for Job's trials and tribulations; Job about the nature of divine justice. God has the last word. And He isn't exactly thrilled with the conversation as the above text shows. In fact, it reminds me of that statement made by Longshanks, the English king in Braveheart, "Who is this person..." we love to quote.

Luckily, nobody was tossed out the window of Job's house. But God does have the final word, and it is a strong rebuke to those who have misrepresented Him and His ways.

Mark 8:22-25

22 They came to Bethsaida. They brought a blind man to him and begged him to touch him.
23 He took the blind man by the hand and brought him out of the village. Spitting on
his eyes and laying his hands on him, he asked him, "Do you see anything?"
24 He looked up and said, "I see people — they look like trees walking."
25 Again Jesus placed his hands on the man's eyes. The man looked intently
and his sight was restored and he saw everything clearly.

I'm struck by Jesus' persistence in this incident. He didn't let an initial failure detract him. His intent was to restore the man's sight completely.

How often a small setback or unforeseen variable sidetracks my good intentions. Sometimes it can be something as little as interruption. I fail to follow through when given an excuse to quit. Not Jesus. He knew His calling. He knew His ability. And he finished His work. Oh to be more like Him.

"Lord, give me the grace this day and in the days to come to finish the course and complete the work You have for me to do."

Ezekiel 11:19-20

Here is what God desires Christian families and churches to look like:

> 19 "I will give them integrity off heart and put a new spirit within them; I will remove their heart of stone from their bodies and give them a heart of flesh,
> 20 "so that they will follow my statutes, keep my ordinances, and practice them. They will be my people, and I will be their God.

Follow the Lord Jesus Christ. Keep in step with the Holy Spirit. Practice the life of holiness that pleases the Lord in every good work.

Three responses that God desires from His people.

John at Everest Base Camp

Psalm 38:1

"LORD, do not punish me in your anger or discipline me in your wrath."

Wait to discipline children until the anger for what they have done passes. That's what timeout is for; to let the emotions of the moment subside. Timeout is for parents so the discipline that follows is appropriate to the offense committed.

Some of the times I most regret as a parent was letting my anger influence the discipline my children needed. Overreaction. Anger is rarely helpful. As James says, it doesn't bring about the righteous life that God desires. (James 1:20)

Psalms 101:1-2

We are attending church service with Jared and the boys this morning in Greensboro. Jared is leading the worship time at Christ Church. Some thoughts from another worship leader to perhaps set a tone today.

> *1 I will sing of faithful love and justice; I will sing praise to you, LORD.*
> *2 I will pay attention to the way of integrity. When will you come to*
> *me? I will live with a heart of integrity in my house.*

Three wonderful biblical qualities; faithful love, justice, integrity. Taken together they provide a framework for parents, spouses, church members - so many of the relationships we live out.

Consider the first. Faithful love contrasts with fickle or episodic love. It is constant love that isn't conditional. It is foundational. This type of love is the foundation we build marriage and family on. Its source is, God, who is love.

"I will sing praise to You, LORD."

Justice is how we respond to contentious or conflict situations. From the platform of faithful love our goal should be doing what is right for others. Justice is the administration of righteousness (the same root word). It is weighing carefully our response and actions to others, always taking their best interest into primary consideration.

That may involve speaking truth in love, exercising tough love to correct and using other means of discipline. But always with patience, kindness, humility.

Add to faithful love and justice the third element, integrity. It reinforces faithful love since it captures the idea of being wholesome. An integer in math is the whole number, something without division. Having that genuine quality others rely on makes the administration of justice as a parent, a spouse, a neighbor effective and acceptable.

Love, justice and integrity. See what our Lord models for us and calls us to! What a wonderful life He fashions for His followers.

"I will sing praise to You, LORD."

Proverbs 16:18

"Pride comes before destruction, and an arrogant spirit before a fall."

Another one of those gems from Solomon's guide to better living. How often we see it at play on the sports fields. It was one of the lessons I taught each of my sons because of their prowess in sports.

Proverbs 16:24

"Pleasant words are a honeycomb: sweet to the taste and health to the body."

I remember the delicious birthday dinner with birthday honors at Jared and Brooke's house. The table was full of wonderful tastes and the room filled with pleasant, encouraging, happy conversation. A real 16:24 holiday for the Matthews family.

Genesis 1:2

*"The earth was without form, and void; and darkness was on the face of the
deep. And the Spirit of God was hovering over the face of the waters."*

Thinking about this great verse at the very outset of all God's revelation to mankind. It is the condition of the cosmos before God inserts His creative design. Two words characterize that cosmos: formless and void. Unstructured, empty. What a description of unredeemed life before God's grace pours in and renews a person. Lacking structure. The absence of a guiding principle/operating system into a *"path of righteousness for His Name's sake."* (Psalm 23:3).

And the emptiness. 17th century philosopher Blaise Pascal said, "There is a God-shaped vacuum in the heart of every person which cannot be filled by any created thing, but only by God, the Creator". The Apostle Paul speaks of the "new creation" that Christ brings. It is all that matters. (Gal 6:15). And, as He did in the first creation, God's initial redemptive move is to insert light. "Let there be light". In redemption, Jesus Himself is that light which floods our chaotic, empty darkness and begins organizing and filling. O what a wonderful Savior! He is that Creator/Redeemer.

Galatians 6:22-23

*22 But the fruit of the Spirit is love, joy, peace, patience, kindness, goodness, faithfulness,
23 gentleness, and self-control. The law is not against such things.*

I have meditated about these nine characteristics of the Spirit-led Life over the years. And one of those traits jumped out this morning, maybe for the first time: gentleness.

Being gentle involves an important assessment of my own strength relative to the other person. It is an inner desire to control that strength in service of the other's good.

Physical use of gentleness is the most obvious application. But what about communication and being gentle with my words? Or emotional gentleness and taking care of the other's emotional state?

Paul makes an immediate application in the first verse of the next chapter:

Galatians 7:1 Brothers and sisters, if someone is overtaken in any wrongdoing, you who are spiritual, restore such a person with a gentle spirit, watching out for yourselves so that you also won't be tempted.

Being gentle in the exercise of correction and discipline.

One writer captured the essence of biblical gentleness in this way: "Sensitivity of disposition and kindness of behavior, founded on strength and prompted by love."

"Holy Spirit produce this wonderful trait in all of our lives to better reflect what You are like and the fruit you bring in us."

Proverbs 8:13

"To fear the LORD is to hate evil. I hate arrogant pride, evil conduct, and perverse speech."

I love the proverbs. They clarify so much in life. We often think wrongly about the fear of the Lord. Here Solomon clarifies exactly what that Holy fear looks like: hating arrogance, bad behavior and corrupt talk. Attitudes, actions and speech guided by a deep respect for God Who sets the standard for these things.

This is something we should practice and teach to our families. When we live humble, godly lives restraining our tongues, we set an example they can follow in the fear of the Lord.

2 Corinthians 7:9-10

9 I now rejoice, not because you were grieved, but because your grief led to repentance. For you were grieved as God willed, so that you didn't experience any loss from us. 10 For godly grief produces a repentance that leads to salvation without regret.

Regret versus repentance. Regret merely condemns and ultimately destroys because it doesn't bring a change of course. It is momentary.

But repentance is a path to change and finally eternal life as it is combined with faith. Paul here encourages us to let regret for our wrongs lead us to repentance .. godly life change.

Psalm 41:9-11

9 Even my friend in whom I trusted, one who ate my bread, has raised his heel against me.
10 But you, LORD, be gracious to me and raise me up; then I will repay them.
11 By this I know that you delight in me: my enemy does not shout in triumph over me.

Three amazing Old Testament prophetic verses in this passage all fulfilled in the life and ministry of Jesus Christ. Here, the betrayal of Judas Iscariot is anticipated and the role it played in Jesus' execution. "One who ate my bread, has raised his heel against me."

It also forecasts His resurrection from the dead. "Be gracious to me and raise me up". And the impact that has on the power of death (our final enemy). Death no longer has the final word for those in Christ Jesus. "My enemy does not shout in triumph over me."

Praise the Lord Jesus for His wonderful redemptive work that offers us the blessed hope of eternal life.

Leviticus 5-7

In this passage, the Lord explains to Moses three sacrifices: sin, guilt and fellowship. As I was pondering these ancient, and seemingly archaic religious exercises a new thought came to me. In the first instance sin must be dealt with in our lives. It is the human condition that separates God from man. Without an accounting for sin, we are at enmity with God. The guilt offering is our accountability. It acknowledges to God that we recognize the sin we have done and that it must be redeemed. Only then can fellowship be resumed with our Creator.

And that fellowship is why the final offering is made. It is a formal re-establishment of relationship with God. It says "my sin created a breakdown that I have acknowledged. Now let's resume our friendship". With the Christian, the entire process is contained in what Jesus did on the cross. He, the Lamb of God, took on Himself the guilt for our sins. Fellowship is established by acknowledging and trusting His redemptive work. Now we deal with sin through 1 John 1:9:

*"If we confess our sins, he is faithful and righteous to forgive us
our sins and cleanse us from all unrighteousness".*

Let's make a full confession to God of any trespass that might have broken fellowship with Him and receive His forgiveness and the restoration of our relationship in Christ.

1 Timothy 2:5

*5 For there is one God and one mediator between God and humanity, the man Christ Jesus,
6 who gave himself as a ransom for all, a testimony at the proper time.*

The Apostle Paul's explanation of the salvation expressed in John 3:16 through Christ is why we need the whole counsel of God to fully appreciate the Christian faith and experience. Apart from the cross, humanity and its Creator are impossibly separated. That chasm required a ransom, a payment for offenses we had committed against Him. Nobody could make that payment for themselves, let alone anybody else because we all had sinned and fallen short of the glory or standard of God's holiness. Enter the Son of God into this dilemma. Paul calls him the mediator, the go-between a holy God and sinful humanity.

There are many mediators in our day. Labor disputes are mediated by attorneys. Political mediators bring hostile sides together. These mediators use facts, logic, reason to their mediations. But Christ was a mediator of an entirely different sort. He made the payment for sin by suffering the penalty we rightly deserved - death on the cross. He paid the penalty for sin that God required and we deserved. His blood was the ransom price that He, and He alone was able to pay. And He was willing. And the Father was willing to accept that payment. Praise God.

That, my dear family, is the most important message we will ever know. That is the gospel, the story of redemption, the core of our faith, the only way to eternal life. Our good works or intentions will never bridge the gap between God and us. Only the cross of Christ and the blood He shed can do that. There is only one mediator, Jesus Christ, who gave Himself as a ransom.

Ezekiel 33:11

"Tell them, 'As I live - this is the declaration of the Lord GOD — I take no pleasure in the death of the wicked, but rather that the wicked person should turn from his way and live. Repent, repent of your evil ways!"

So good to see that even in a prophecy like Ezekiel's where judgment is declared on all the nations, that the attitude of God is for restoration. He wants all people everywhere to repent, to turn from their sins and to trust in His redemptive work through Christ. God hates sin. But neither does He take pleasure in judging sin. He wants all people to turn from their wickedness and be forgiven and restored to fellowship with Him.

Ephesians 2:8

"For it is by grace you are saved through faith."

Thinking about this great truth in the New Testament this morning. Grace is something we all desire. It is unmerited favor. Getting a gift, something we have not earned.

Birthday honors. It is one of our family's precious times of the year for me. We gather on a person's birthday and shower them with verbal gifts about their character, faith, aptitudes, progress .. you name it. It is unearned favor from family members.

With God, the key to unlocking His grace in our lives is faith. That comes more easily for some than for others. Trusting is a very personal thing. But however it is accomplished, it is the only way of seeing God's grace in our lives.

Birthday honors are bestowed in the Matthews family by simply being a member of the family either by birth or marriage. In God's family, grace is achieved solely by faith in the One who grants the grace.

Luke 13:23

An interesting question from **Luke 13** this morning.

*23 "Lord," someone asked him, "are only a few people going to be saved?" He said to them,
24 "Make every effort to enter through the narrow door, because I
tell you, many will try to enter and won't be able."*

That narrow door to salvation opens only on Jesus. There are not many ways to heaven. The door opens only to those who repent and have faith. Admitting I need God isn't easy for a self-righteous person to do. It is an act of humility and self-abnegation.

I have a friend who is not bothered by Jesus, the historical figure and what He taught. He is not opposed to the Christian ethic of loving your neighbor and doing unto others as you would have them do to you. What my friend can't abide is the idea that he is a sinner in need of a Savior.

In our modern age the individual is deified. That cuts against this teaching. Some effort is required. Not to say I can work my way to heaven. Only that I must overcome the obstacles of this age to enter that narrow door.

If only we could see more clearly what is on the other side

Psalm 56:3

"When I am afraid, I will trust in you."

What a little nugget of rich truth contained in this verse! So many different ways to deal with fear. Flight is a common way. Run away! Denial is another way of handling fear. But this way fails to account for the reality that prompts a fearful response.

The psalmist offers a better way, rooted in reality and in deliverance from the power of fear. Trust in the Lord. There is no circumstance beyond His power and knowledge. He is never surprised by any circumstance and isn't overwhelmed by them either. God is able. Just trust. It could be a new motto in times of fear. Just trust.

And here is the conclusion of the Psalmist to his confident trust in the Lord a few verses later.

Psalm 56:13 For you rescued me from death, even my feet from stumbling, to walk before God in the light of life.

Walking in the light of life. Wonderful picture for anyone stumbling through the obstacles of life's doubt and fear.

Luke 18:22

22 When Jesus heard this, he told him, "You still lack one thing: Sell all you have and distribute it to the poor, and you will have treasure in heaven. Then come, follow me."
23 After he heard this, he became extremely sad, because he was very rich.
24 Seeing that he became sad, Jesus said, "How hard it is for those who have wealth to enter the kingdom of God!

Here is the account of a man who seeks after Christ but carries baggage (wealth) that hinders him from embracing Jesus. The Lord makes it clear to him (and to us) that our "stuff" can be a barrier to following Jesus. We are wealthy in a comparative sense. We aren't wealthy like the president. I don't even have the wealth of my parents. But we have an abundance compared to much of the world.

As I thought about this I found two key attitudes/practices that will keep our wealth from being a barrier to close relationship with Christ. Generosity is the first. Thankfulness is the other. As we cultivate these two things, we may avoid the trap of idolatry that wealth can bring.

Psalm 75:6

6 Exaltation does not come from the east, the west, or the desert,
7 for God is the Judge: He brings down one and exalts another.

And He does so in perfect judgment for God weighs not only actions but motives and His judgments are true. In fact they are beautiful and praiseworthy. The judgment of God is rarely preached or even mentioned in our age of grace. But it is a consistent theme and truth expressed throughout scripture beginning in the judgment of Adam and Eve and ending in the judgments of Revelation on both the fallen angelic and human realms.

Truth be told, we like that, because we are made in God's image with the capacity to judge. Inwardly we want truth and righteousness rewarded and evil and error punished. It starts in our families with the children. We train them using judgments about their character and actions. And we do the same with each other. But while we gladly exercise our own judgments, how often do we reject the right of the Ultimate Judge to exercise His. When He seems to fail in His judgments (evil winning over good) we criticize Him or even deny He exists. When His judgments seem too strict, (Thou shalt not ... fill in the blank) we make excuse for our wrong behavior rather than submitting to Him.

(To be continued)

Psalm 75:7

".. for God is the Judge: He brings down one and exalts another."

God is the Judge. At the Decision America event in Portland, Oregon in 2018, Franklin Graham spoke on the judgments of God. He pulled no punches. He labeled the things God will judge .. lying, stealing, murder, idolatry, greed, lust and even things like cowardice. For many in that crowd of 12,000+ it might have been the first time anybody had clearly and biblically outlined the way God the Judge will evaluate mankind's wicked behaviors and attitudes. And, of course, the Good News is that God poured out His righteous indignation (that is a powerful phrase) on His only begotten Son at the cross so that by aligning ourselves with Christ by faith, we can avoid divine judgment and the wrath to come.

I have rarely seen a large crowd so focused on a message. There was little stirring in that mass audience as the message of God's judgments and His perfect plan of redemption was clearly presented. Hundreds responded to the call Franklin made to get right with this Righteous God by trusting in His Son as Savior/Redeemer. It was wonderful. As we worship today, take a moment to thank Him for sending His Son as the atoning sacrifice for our sin - my sin, your sin. And for giving us the great hope of the Gospel we can share with our families and others.

Ephesians 4: 1

1 Therefore I, the prisoner in the Lord, urge you to live worthy of the calling you have received,
2 with all humility and gentleness, with patience, bearing with one another in love,
3 making every effort to keep the unity of the Spirit through the bond of peace

Paul asks a question (or implies one) that every Christian ought to ask. What does a Christian life look like?

And his answer in these three verses is transformative. A life worthy of the name Christ follower is:

- humble
- gentle with others
- patient in adversity
- bearing each others burdens in love
- striving for unity with others
- and peaceable.

Doesn't that define what "loving your neighbor as yourself" actually looks like?
May the Lord give us wisdom and inner strength to be that sort of people.

Isaiah 54: 13

13 Then all your children will be taught by the LORD, their prosperity will be great,
14 and you will be established on a foundation of righteousness.

Thinking a lot today about passing things on to the following generations. Not so long ago, I spent the final hours with my mother as she crossed over into the life to come. It is a life-altering experience.

I want to leave behind a good inheritance for my sons and their families. But here in these verses is the more precious wealth to be passed on, the foundation of righteousness. Prosperity without it is an empty, passing thing. Wealth devoid of worship has little if any value.

So I add to that pursuit of material wealth the desire to be a man rich in faith. An example to my family as a Christian. That must begin with the way I treat Gwen. It is my primary witness in this world to the love of Christ.

Then my Christian witness extends into the way I treat my extended family and finally my neighbors. These are the measures of righteousness by which God evaluates me. May He receive the glory as I measure up to His standard to *"Love the Lord your God with all your heart, soul, and mind. And love your neighbor as yourself."* Matthew 22:37,39

John 8:21

The worst thing that could happen to a person Jesus warns about in this passage. In fact, He emphasizes it three times as He contends with His opponents, the Pharisees.

> 21 Then he said to them again, *"I'm going away; you will look for me, and you will die in your sin. Where I'm going, you cannot come."*
> 22 So the Jews said again, *"He won't kill himself, will he, since he says, 'Where I'm going, you cannot come'?"*
> 23 *"You are from below,"* he told them, *"I am from above. You are of this world; I am not of this world.*
> 24 *"Therefore I told you that you will die in your sins. For if you do not believe that I am he, you will die in your sins."*

"You will die in your sins." It is the worst fate that can befall a person. And Jesus came to save people from that most awful and eternal condition.

1 John 1:9 offers the remedy for this most awful fate of dying in my sins.

> *"If we confess our sins He is faithful and just to forgive us our sins and to purify us from all unrighteousness."*

This is the gospel of our Lord Jesus Christ.

Psalm 45:4

*"In your splendor ride triumphantly in the cause of truth, humility,
and justice. May your right hand show your awe-inspiring acts."*

Have you ever wondered what the government, civic affairs and the political discourse will look like when Jesus Christ returns and establishes His reign on earth for 1000 years?

This verse gives us the basis for his government. It is not liberty. It is not equality. It is not "from each according to his ability to each according to his need", the Communist/Socialist creed.

Jesus' reign will be marked by these three great attributes so sorely missing in our world .. truth, humility and justice. Let those concepts sink in. Let them interact in your meditation. See how they will transform everything in the public dialogue in that day.

And it will be under-girded by His awesome, limitless power to act.

Come Lord Jesus!

Ruth 2:4

*"Later, when Boaz arrived from Bethlehem, he said to the harvesters, 'The
LORD be with you.' 'The LORD bless you,' they replied."*

This encounter takes placed during one of Israel's lowest historical eras spiritually: the time of Judges. But there were faithful people there too. And this greeting captures the attitudes of those people, one of whom was Boaz. Here he encounters his field hands working the harvest.

Two things are requested of God in this exchange: Gods presence and His blessing. What a wonderful expression in an otherwise corrupt condition where following God's commands were rare. During this time we are told that people did what was right in their own eyes. Not unlike the culture we live in.

Good to know that regardless of how bad society strays from the truth there are always opportunities to respond in a godly way

John 9:8

"I believe, Lord!" he said, and he worshiped him.

This miracle where Jesus gives sight to a man born blind is quite thrilling. As the man himself says, "Who has ever given sight to someone blind from birth?" He was defending Jesus in front of the Pharisees who were using this miracle to further accuse Jesus. But the man's response is what caught my eye this morning. The text says he believed and he worshipped.

That is the nature of faith. It always yields worship. It is the natural outgrowth of belief; worship and praise. It is the outward expression of an inward attitude. As we go to church on Sunday, it is good to remember why we do that. Worship is the visible expression of an inner conviction.

"I believe."

Therefore, I worship. Just like this man whose sight was restored.

Galatians 2:19-21

Here is the great summation of Christian conversion as given by The Apostle Paul to the church at Galatia.

19 I have been crucified with Christ,
20 and I no longer live, but Christ lives in me. The life I now live in the body I
live by faith in the Son of God, who loved me and gave Himself for me.
21 I do not set aside the grace of God, for if righteousness comes
through the law, then Christ died for nothing.

The sweetest words that reach my heart this morning are these; "who loved me, and gave Himself for me."

This is the greatest love, the kind that self-sacrifices. That was the love of the cross where Jesus paid the debt for my sins that I could never pay.

"Greater love has no one than this, that one lays down his life for his friends."
John 15:13

What a wonderful Savior!

Jeremiah 11:22-23

22 Therefore, this is what the LORD of Hosts says: "I am about to punish them. The young men will die by the sword; their sons and daughters will die by famine.
23 They will have no remnant, for I will bring disaster on the people of Anathoth in the year of their punishment."

What is one of the greatest assets I possess? My home? My money or my possessions? Not according to this verse. It is my offspring, my children and grandchildren.

The final level of Gods judgment is to wipe away any trace of a person from the future. That is his offspring, his family. It clearly shows what is of highest value, the things that endure. May it never be in this family. May we be a God-loving and God-fearing family for generations to come.

Four Generations with GrammaLou

John 1:14

*"The Word became flesh and dwelt among us. We observed his glory, the glory
as the one and only Son from the Father, full of grace and truth."*

I was raised in a little Northeast Portland church, a Plymouth Brethren Assembly, called Grace and Truth Gospel Hall. In that little church, Scripture was hung on nearly every wall and painted on some of the rafters. It was a "truth" based place and did a good job of training its people the precepts of God. I'm thankful for that biblical foundation.

But the truth of G&T was sometimes not balanced by the grace of its name. Truth calls out sin, grace gives God's path to redemption which starts and ends at the cross. Jesus died to take the punishment and guilt of my sin. Grace and Truth church did a wonderful job of reminding us about God's grace expressed through the sacrifice of His Son. We had a weekly remembrance service focused on Jesus' sacrifice called the Breaking of Bread. It was communion.

Living out that grace by waiting on God to complete His work in our lives is the tension we often experience. We want to judge the sin in others rather than letting God do His job. I want grace and truth on my timeline. That makes me a little too quick to judge .. a little impatient to wait on the Holy Spirit to do His sanctifying work. I correct more and pray less. Thus, I take on the look of the legalistic Pharisee who Jesus strongly opposed.

Grace and Truth is a balance best struck by Christ than by us. Living out Grace and Truth is trusting God to work out my salvation, your salvation. Having an attitude of fear and trembling as that sanctification takes place is how God asks me to respond.

1 Samuel 22:2

*"In addition, every man who was desperate, in debt, or discontented rallied around
him, and he became their leader. About 400 men were with him."*

King David's collection of loyal men while he was in exile is interesting. Actually, these guys were desperados as here described by their character qualities. Desperation. Debt. Discontentment. The Bible is filled with such characters, too. The stories of Scripture don't read like heroic fables designed to validate a cultural myth. Rather, the pages are filled with fallible, fallen men and women in need of the redemptive work of God in their lives.

It is why I relate so well to the Bible. The sort of people I find in its pages are similar to me .. desperate at times, struggling with debt and often discontent.

2 Samuel 13:15

"So Amnon hated Tamar with such intensity that the hatred he hated her with was greater than the love he had loved her with. 'Get out of here!' he said."

This is one of Scripture's most lurid and troubling stories. It is the evidence that even in a Bible hero like David, not all is perfection. Far from it, especially in his family! All the more reason to pray continually for our family members!

And Tuesday is that day we focus on each other for God to work His grace and mercy in our lives. But back to Amnon and Tamar. The lesson is this: sin never truly satisfies. Here is the immoral actions of Amnon toward his half sister. He is attracted to her in a way proscribed by the Law of Moses. That is sin. But for this young man, the one and only concern is satisfying his lust. He cares nothing for his sister (obviously), his parents, other family members. It's just about him and his desires.

Pursuing lust is the ultimate tunnel-vision. Amnon shows us how destructive the pursuit of lust can be. It divides his family and ultimately destroys his own life. Absalom, the brother of the sister Amnon rapes eventually gets revenge by killing him. But what struck me was what Amnon actually derived from this moment of lustful insanity. He burned with passion for Tamar, but as soon as he satisfied his lust his appetite turned to derision, even hatred. What evidence of the folly of chasing sinful passion for our satisfaction!

God promises to fulfill our deepest desires with good things. He possesses a storehouse of ultimate satisfaction, something the lusts of the flesh can never provide. God's provisions never carry regret or division or destruction. They are genuinely wholesome and satisfying. Our world sends us constant messaging to taste of its illicit lusts. It comes in media, on television and film, in popular music. But what the world offers is empty. It will never satisfy and in the end it leaves only the "Amnon-curse" behind.

Psalm 34:8 *Taste and see that the LORD is good. How happy is the person who takes refuge in him!*

Psalm 42:8

"The LORD will send his faithful love by day; his song will be with me in the night —a prayer to the God of my life."

I woke up this morning with a hymn coursing through my mind. It is one of the delightful experiences being awakened in the morning with a hymn of praise to God.

It set me to thinking about how I prepare myself for those 7-8 hours of sleep when my mind wanders off in dreams. We spend a third of our lives in that subconscious state. I have been in that dream world for more than 20 years already, with hopefully many more to come (a not so subtle reminder my birthday is coming up!). Wouldn't it be good to commit these hours to God and let Him direct our dream-life?

When Jared was a young boy he went through a period when nightmares oppressed him at night. I remember praying each night with him that God would come, fill his room with His presence and direct every thought to His praise and glory.

"O God, bring me a song tonight, a prayer to you in my life."

2 Chronicles 15:7

"But as for you, be strong; don't give up, for your work has a reward."

Be strong. Don't give up. Reward coming.

Marriage is hard work. Blending two separate personalities into a one (the two become one, as Scripture says) is not a Sunday walk in the park. There are challenges and conflicts. It is difficult. Maybe that is what makes a long term marriage so rewarding. Huge investment.

I value few things more than Gwen. It wasn't always that way. But sometime around the 15th year of marriage she surpassed Duck football in my estimation. (That's mostly a joke!) And what about raising kids. That needs endurance. Strength. Persistence. But when you get to this stage of grand parenting, all of it takes on a new meaning. It bridges from the immediate present to the future hope a family can give. That's a unique perspective that only comes through work, persistence and refusing to give up.

There is a great reward in seeing your children raising their children. Career. Serving the Lord. Neighborliness. The list can go on. Strength. Persistence. Reward. Excellent advice for a fulfilling life

1 Samuel 16:7

"But the LORD said to Samuel, 'Do not look at his appearance or at his physical stature, because I have refused him. For the LORD does not see as man sees; for man looks at the outward appearance, but the LORD looks at the heart."

Confession time. This verse sends small shudders through me. I know what my heart can be like. I don't want God, or anyone else looking at the content of my heart. It is often black! Jeremiah defines my heart in that famous verse *"The heart is deceitful above all things and desperately wicked. Who can know it?"* Jeremiah 17:9. I'm glad none of you can see the things that pass through this black heart. But God does.

This is where dark hearts can take comfort in the spiritual journey of a man like David .. who it is said "he was a man after God's heart". David had his black heart moments too. Bathsheba? And how he tried to hide his sin by having her husband slain on the battlefield. It was from that incident that he wrote the great 51st Psalm, one of the greatest examples of heart-felt repentance in not just the Bible but all literature. In that Psalm, David gives black-hearted people the hope we need to press on in pursuit of godliness.

Psalm 51:10 *Create in me a clean heart, O God, and renew a steadfast spirit within me.*

We live in an already/not yet condition. In Christ, God somehow sees me as a finished spiritual product with a clean heart. But from my perspective, that's not even close. For God I am already. For me, not yet. That leads me to David's prayer in Psalm 51.

"Lord, finish the work You began so many years ago. Create in me that clean heart and steadfast spirit You desire and require for eternal life with You."

Colossians 1:9-12

The Apostle Paul was perhaps the first and greatest disciple-maker in the early church. He planted churches all around the Roman world and followed up on their progress in the faith to insure that a Christian presence would live beyond his ministry. Considering the worldwide impact that the gospel has had in the past two millennia, I would say Paul did a spectacular job of training those first century, Gentile Christians.

In the preamble to his pastoral letter to the church in Colossae, Paul offers us the spiritual checklist he worked through in those first century churches. It is a good list to measure my progress in the faith in this distant corner of history. Some things never change!

9 For this reason we also, since the day we heard it, do not cease to pray for you, and to ask that
you may be filled with the knowledge of His will in all wisdom and spiritual understanding;
10 that you may walk worthy of the Lord, fully pleasing Him, being fruitful
in every good work and increasing in the knowledge of God;
11 strengthened with all might, according to His glorious power,
for all patience and longsuffering with joy;
12 giving thanks to the Father who has qualified us to be partakers
of the inheritance of the saints in the light.

Here is Paul's checklist for a disciple:

1. Wisdom and spiritual understanding to pursue God's will in my life.
2. A Christian walk worthy of the One who died for me.
3. A desire to please God.
4. Doing good works that bear fruit.
5. Growing in the knowledge of God.

6.   Being strengthened by God for the character of patience in trials, and even finding joy in them.

7.   Thankfulness for what is to come because of God's promises.

Whew! I'm exhausted. But also challenged. Which is one of Scripture's main purposes: to both encourage AND challenge me in the faith. And the Apostle Paul was a master at that.

Colossians 1:15-20

I would be remiss to leave the list from yesterday without a proper context. Yes, it is a daunting task to be Jesus' follower. That list of what Paul expected in a disciple is no joke! But in the following verses Paul puts into context what Christ has done to make all that possible. This is the "wow" factor:

15 He is the image of the invisible God, the firstborn over all creation.
16 For by Him all things were created that are in heaven and that are on
earth, visible and invisible, whether thrones or dominions or principalities
or powers. All things were created through Him and for Him.
17 And He is before all things, and in Him all things consist.
18 And He is the head of the body, the church, who is the beginning, the firstborn
from the dead, that in all things He may have the preeminence.
19 For it pleased the Father that in Him all the fullness should dwell,
20 and by Him to reconcile all things to Himself, by Him, whether things on earth
or things in heaven, having made peace through the blood of His cross.

The "heavy lifting" was done by Christ. My response is simple faith that produces obedience.

Proverbs 10:3

Here's an excellent piece of wisdom for today's meditation:

"The LORD will not let the righteous go hungry, but he denies the wicked what they crave."

In other words, it's a 'needs' vs. 'wants' thing. Wise people have their needs met by the Lord. That is their focus. Foolish people are chasing their wants and they are never satisfied.

Exodus 18:21

"Moreover you shall select from all the people able men, such as fear God, men of truth, hating covetousness; and place such over them to be rulers of thousands, rulers of hundreds, rulers of fifties, and rulers of tens."

Okay, this is entirely too political for a daily devotion, but here goes. It is hard in our secular, post-modern world to find biblical commitments in the culture. When we do, we should rejoice that there is something left of the rapidly crumbling Judeo-Christian culture bequeathed to us. From Exodus we have the picture of a leader with three qualities. Good for us to support these qualities in our leaders when we find them.

1. God fearing - steer away from secularists. Mike Pence is a good example of such a god-fearing person. So was Joe Lieberman, just to be fair and balanced!

2. Men of truth - not only people who defend truth, but also practice it. We have suffered as a nation recently in our highest offices from men and women who deny truth. "Read my lips. No new taxes!" "I did not have sexual relations with that woman Lewinsky." "Weapons of mass destruction in Iraq." "If you like your insurance, you can keep your insurance." Our current President also seems truth challenged. Finding a truthful and truth-filled person would be a marked improvement in the future.

3. Hatred of covetousness. Financial corruption in high office is rampant. It goes beyond politics into business, entertainment and even the church.

Interesting how of all the deadly sins that could have been mentioned in disqualifying a leader, Jethro chose this one. The attitude of a covetous person is what leads to corruption. Wouldn't we love to live under the leadership of a Moses whose main fault seems to be trying to do too much (why his father-in-Law had this little discussion with him) rather than finding ways of corrupting the God-given leadership entrusted to him.

Proverbs 1:5

We enter one of my favorite books of the Bible this morning, Proverbs. It is the pinnacle of wisdom literature, not just in Scripture but in all literature. And this morning a verse about becoming and being wise really jumped out at me.

"A wise man will hear and increase learning, And a man of understanding will attain wise counsel."

Being able to discern or hear wisdom is the starting point. Closing my ears to what wisdom teaches inhibits its acquisition and growth in my life. Attaining that wisdom, capturing it and not letting its lessons evaporate is another key to the wise person. How often I heard my mother say to me, "how many times must I tell you!" That is the way of the fool, not the wise person: always hearing but never acquiring. Failing to do.

Combine acquisition with attainment and we arrive at increasing wisdom, the place most people really want to be. Here is the mature person, moving from one stage of life to the next. Lessons received then learned result in a life well-lived and growing. The beauty of biblical wisdom.

"Lord, give me eyes and ears to perceive wisdom's call this day. And grant me the heart to obey its direction that I may be a man of wisdom for Your service."

Genesis 39:7-9

*7 And it came to pass after these things that his master's wife cast
longing eyes on Joseph, and she said, "Lie with me."
8 But he refused and said to his master's wife, "Look, my master does not know what
is with me in the house, and he has committed all that he has to my hand.
9 "There is no one greater in this house than I, nor has he kept back anything from me but you,
because you are his wife. How then can I do this great wickedness, and sin against God?"*

This incident in the life of Joseph is one of the more famous stories of all scripture. And as we hear

Joseph deflect from the immoral wishes of his Egyptian master's wife, there is a good lesson about living a holy life for us. Joseph recounts for this woman all the trust her husband has placed in him. But when he gets to the bottom line of why he won't engage in an adulterous affair with her it is this: how can he do this, for it would be a sin not against Potiphar but against God.

Isn't that the key to living a holy life? Recognizing that when I sin, it is first God who I offend. My actions surely have an impact on others - family, friends, colleagues - but offending them alone is not enough to control the beast within. The greater restraint is the fear of the Lord.

Job 33:24

"Then He is gracious to him, and says, 'Deliver him from going down to the Pit; I have found a ransom'."

This is the final argument levied against Job in this long examination of why a righteous man would suffer. Job lost everything but his life. And his "friends" tried to convince him that it was because God punishes sin, his sin. As this young man enters the conversation, he makes a point with centuries of implication. It is a prophetic statement that would be revealed to the world in Christ.

Without a ransom for our sins and transgression, we are headed for eternal destruction.

He misapplied Job's extreme misfortunes as that ransom. We know that wasn't the case. In fact God used Job to demonstrate to the angelic world the power of one man's faith in Him. But in this verse Elihu offers a great truth for us to revel in: God found a ransom for our sin. We have all sinned and fallen short of His glory. But God's purpose in redeeming sinful man from the eternal consequence of sin was fulfilled when His one and only Son became our ransom for sin. Jesus paid it all on the cross. Every offense I have committed he covered by shedding his blood. The ransom for my sin is met. I am redeemed from eternal judgment. Praise the Lord Jesus Christ!

Isaiah 43:10-12

10 *"You are My witnesses," says the LORD, "And My servant whom I have chosen, That you may know and believe Me, And understand that I am He. Before Me there was no God formed, Nor shall there be after Me. 11 I, even I, am the LORD, And besides Me there is no savior. 12 I have declared and saved, I have proclaimed, And there was no foreign god among you; Therefore you are My witnesses," Says the LORD, "that I am God.*

This is an amazing set of verses from Isaiah. It is God speaking to us about His plan to reveal Himself to the world. He has chosen us as the instrument of witnessing for Him. So I ask, "How can I witness to the reality of God my Savior? What does my life reveal about the redemptive power of God? The passage speaks about knowing and believing in Him. Good place to start. Do I know God or only know about Him? Am I in a personal relationship with God my Savior? Do we talk? Do I respond? He loves me! Do I return His love?

And do I take this personal relationship to others as a witness for Him. I readily tell other people about my wife. I tell them about my children and grandchildren too. That is a part of having an active relationship. Is it the same with God? This passage is God speaking directly to us. If we know Him and believe in Him, we are called to be His witnesses.

Mark 5:19

"However, Jesus did not permit him, but said to him, 'Go home to your friends, and tell them what great things the Lord has done for you, and how He has had compassion on you."

This is the story of the man possessed by a "legion" of demons. That's a whole bunch of evil possession that Jesus freed him from. The man's encounter with the Lord gave him a powerful testimony to tell others. Interesting how the Word from two different passages takes me to witnessing for Christ: yesterday in Isaiah, today in Mark.

The topic of witness today is how Jesus releases us from our spiritual chains. Those could be chains of addiction or bitterness or regrets. They could be emotional, physical or spiritual, as in this case. Chains that bind me into a place of misery, like this man. It is a lonely, desperate place. Jesus came to set us free. And as free people, we have a testimony the world, our friends and neighbors need to hear.

"Lord, let me revel this day in all the ways you have given me freedom and provide the opportunities to tell others about that wonderful release."

Mark 11:24-25

24 *"Therefore I say to you, whatever things you ask when you pray,*
believe that you receive them, and you will have them.
25 *"And whenever you stand praying, if you have anything against anyone, forgive*
him, that your Father in heaven may also forgive you your trespasses.

Jesus makes two conditions for successful prayer in these two verses. The first is faith. When I ask the Lord for something, it must be done knowing and trusting that God hears my prayer and that He can answer it. Praying without faith is an exercise of worry and, by extension, that inner conversation we often have with ourselves. But having that discussion with God and trusting in His ability to answer .. now that is prayer!

Jesus further warns that there is a barrier to successful prayer .. unforgiveness. Harboring a grudge or holding an offense against someone will block God's willingness to answer my prayers. In fact, it's even worse than that. Jesus says in verse 25 that my unwillingness to release others from their offenses against me will cause God to not cancel my offenses against Him. That is serious business. So when we pray, a good place to start is in confession. Ask the Lord, "Am I holding onto an offense against anyone?" That will release the grace of God to pour out on me and also to cover whatever I ask of Him.

2 Corinthians 5:17, 21

17 Therefore, if anyone is in Christ, he is a new creation; old things
have passed away; behold, all things have become new.
21 For He made Him who knew no sin to be sin for us, that we
might become the righteousness of God in Him.

Two wonderful verses of Scripture that define the Gospel of Jesus Christ. First it is a new start. In Christ, a person is a new creation. Born again by the Spirit through the work of Jesus Christ on Calvary. I am that new creation through faith in Him.

But I am also becoming the righteousness of God (verse 21). I am. And I am becoming. Important to keep both things in mind. As a new creation - like a new born baby - I have all kinds of unrealized potential. I was watching Rilynn, our granddaughter, pull herself up on her mother's pant leg yesterday as she begins to explore the potential of walking, then running, then leaping, then spinning and twirling in years to come. Maybe someday this grandpa will attend one of her ballet recitals! But she isn't quite there yet on her pointe shoes.

The same with us in Christ. I'm in Him; fully His child and follower. But not yet manifesting His level of righteous living. That is a "becoming" thing. It is where he wants me to be tomorrow and next year. He wants to attend my "recital" of godliness. But in the meantime, there are lessons to learn, growth to achieve, strength to gain. So I pull myself up on His strong foundation and totter about. Just like little Rilynn in her progress toward ballerina.

Psalm 57:7-11

7 My heart is steadfast, O God, my heart is steadfast; I will sing and give praise.
8 Awake, my glory! Awake, lute and harp! I will awaken the dawn.
9 I will praise You, O Lord, among the peoples; I will sing to You among the nations.
10 For Your mercy reaches unto the heavens, And Your truth unto the clouds.
11 Be exalted, O God, above the heavens; Let Your glory be above all the earth.

In my Scripture reading program, Sunday is set aside for the Psalms. And this 57th Psalm is a good reason to have the Psalms as the section of Scripture read on our traditional day of worship.

Being steadfast in worship of God is a right starting place. How easy to slip away from this weekly discipline with other Christians. And this call to awaken is exactly my need. Easy to fall asleep in my worship life .. to let the cares of this world crowd out the Presence who always abides. I need to be awakened by the Spirit so that praise ushers from my lips to The Father, to Jesus.

And here are three things David commends for worship today:

God's mercy - how often did I fall short of His glory this week, yet He beckons me to come back in worship.

God's truth - here is the solid rock I can stand on that our pastor will unfold for me.

God's glory - what I want to experience this day as my heart, mind and mouth join others to express His praises.

Easter Sunday in Greensboro, 2019

Mark 14:21

Have you ever been betrayed? It still stings decades later. How about forsaken.. abandoned. Hard to get over that. Or denied and falsely accused. These are some of the most agonizing experiences a person must endure. Imagine each of these offenses happening within hours. That was the agony of the Lord Jesus on one terrible, grief-filled night.

21 "The Son of Man indeed goes just as it is written of Him, but woe to that man by whom the Son of Man is betrayed! It would have been good for that man if he had never been born.
50 Then they all forsook Him and fled.
57 Then some rose up and bore false witness against Him 71 Then he began to curse and swear, "I do not know this Man of whom you speak!"

A dark night indeed, perhaps the darkest night of all history. It has given me a new appreciation for His suffering for my sin. His physical torment was only part of it; the mental part was even worse. Denial. Betrayal. Lies. But there were heroes on this darkest of nights.

(To be continued.)

Mark 15:40-41

The darkest of all nights preceded what would become the brightest of dawns. And it was the women who ushered it in.

41 There were also women looking on from afar, among whom were Mary Magdalene, Mary the mother of James the Less and of Joses, and Salome, 41 who also followed Him and ministered to Him when He was in Galilee, and many other women who came up with Him to Jerusalem.

The women! They didn't forsake, betray, deny or falsely accuse. They held fast. And in His darkest hour, they held the light of authentic relationship.

Thank God for the women. As their reward, they were the first to encounter the greatest miracle .. resurrection.

Mark 16:2 *Very early in the morning, on the first day of the week, they came to the tomb when the sun had risen ...*

"Lord, you have blessed me with such wonderful women: Gwen, my mother, my daughters-in-law. So thankful for the women."

Jeremiah 16:5

"For thus says the LORD: Do not enter the house of mourning, or go to lament or grieve for them, for I have taken away my peace from this people, my steadfast love and mercy, declares the LORD."

Israel had come to the point in this prophet's ministry that judgment was certain. God was ready to exile the nation from their homes and lands for 70 years because of their disobedience.

Removing them from their "stuff" was one thing. Withholding His peace, His love and His mercy was another. That would be their greatest loss. Don't we rely totally on those qualities in our God? The peace that passes understanding. The love that "so loved the world". And the mercy that forgives, cleanses and forgets our transgressions when we sin. What would I exchange for God's peace, love and mercy?

So thankful this morning that I bask in the Father's peace, love and mercy.

Book of Ruth

The book of Ruth is one of my favorites in the Bible. It captures what life is like in chaotic, ungodly times for godly people. The story of Ruth and Naomi takes place in the latter years of the times of Judges, a 250 period of Israel's history characterized by the statement, "everyone did what was right in their own eyes." They did not follow the guidance of Scripture. Life became more and more evil and bizarre. But not for everybody.

In the story of Ruth we see a good man, Boaz, caring for the needy, for impoverished relatives (Naomi, Ruth), fulfilling his biblical obligations. He wasn't swayed by the chaos around him. He remained faithful. Further, we see the fidelity of a young woman, Ruth, to self-sacrificial care of her mother-in-law, despite being of a different nationality and culture. Ruth had to uproot from her extended family in Moab to care for Naomi when they returned to Bethlehem. She had no prospects for family, security, possessions. She accepted the destitution of Naomi and all that would entail.

Read the four chapters; it takes less than 15 minutes. It is a sweet narrative after a rough beginning. And it encourages me to remain faithful to the calling of God regardless how chaotic and evil society becomes. There is always room for the faithful. And there is great reward in remaining faithful to God. Through his obedience Boaz would be the great grandpa of Israel's greatest leader, King David.

Luke 3:22

"And the Holy Spirit descended in bodily form like a dove upon Him, and a voice came from heaven which said, 'You are My beloved Son; in You I am well pleased."

At the beginning of Luke's gospel, the author documents the launch of Jesus' public ministry, a three year period that changed the world. Not only did Jesus demonstrate for humanity what God intended for us to be like, He made it possible for us to return to the Father by completing His redemptive work on the cross. At the outset of this public display of grace, God placed His divine approval on the work of His Son. "You are my beloved Son; in You I am well pleased."

This affirmation of the Father is a crucial element as the Son begins His work. Despite everything that He will face, Jesus had this assurance at the outset that He is loved and cherished. It is the power of a father's blessing.

A father's blessing is seen throughout scripture. Abraham blessed Isaac who blessed Jacob and Esau (although the latter's blessing wasn't "all that"). At the close of Genesis we see Jacob twice bless each of his 12 sons. There is something life-defining about a parents blessing of their children. It empowers them. It launches their capabilities. It helps define their direction. Especially when a parent has carefully observed, then affirmed their child's unique qualities.

There is too little of this happening in our day. Our cities have become dangerous places because fathers are absent and children are not raised with this life-defining affirmation. Without the blessings of their fathers, young men set their own course, often tragically

As I look back on my parenting, I wish I had blessed more and corrected less. Correction is crucial in raising a child, but so is blessing. Looking for the special traits, gifts and abilities of our children, then affirming them is at the heart of what Jesus heard from the Father that day in the waters of the Jordan River.

"You are My beloved Son; in You I am well pleased."

Jared and boys, Winter, 2018

Luke 8:31

"And they begged him not to command them to depart into the abyss."

Here is an amazing and really terrifying statement I had never seen until this morning's reading in Luke. Jesus had just cast a legion of demons (dozens of them) from a man. He is freed from their oppression. Now they are without a host to possess. So they beg Jesus not to end their existence just then. These fallen angels know what their eventual and eternal fate will be. It has been revealed in Scripture and the demonic world knows Scripture.

Their end is the abyss. It is perdition. Total separation from God and everything associated with Him. Light. Beauty. Form. Substance. Hell is like the eternal black hole we hear astrophysicists hypothesize about. And these demons want absolutely no part of that reality. So they beg Jesus not to send them there.

I had never realized how averse to hell the demonic world is. I always assumed the devil and his minions were anticipating that as their final, evil bash. Their time when a demonic ethic of evil reigned supreme and they didn't have to contend with the righteous or the goodness of their Creator. Not so. They want no part of that Godless place. And even though they oppose God to their very core, and absolutely hate everything He is and stands for, this side is infinitely better than the blackness of the one to come for them. So they begged.

Hell is the place reserved for those implacably opposed to God. It is fashioned for demons and the devil. But, tragically, humans will also inhabit this place of eternal death. That should be a very sobering thought. And it should motivate me to fully engage with others about hell; to let them know there is an escape from this terrifying, eternal reality. The Gospel gives us that escape path. ".. that whosoever believes on Him shall not perish, but have everlasting life." That option is not available to the fallen spirits. But it is to us. Take the option. Tell others too. The alternative is just too awful to risk as these demons have shown us today.

Proverbs 14:22

"Do they not go astray who devise evil? But mercy and truth belong to those who devise good."

When Jason was a young boy, I tried to read to him from the Proverbs at night. Such a wonderful book of solid teaching in practical ways. But often they capture the core of grace theology. This proverb highlights a wonderful balance we are wise to consider ... mercy and truth. God is willing to extend mercy to whoever calls on His Name. But the condition for divine mercy is truth. I can't sweep my sin under the carpet. I must acknowledge it, name it before the Righteous Judge. Only then does He grant me mercy. It is God's way. He is a Father. He is a Savior. He is also a Judge.

The amazing thing about our God is that He addresses transgressions of His law with His wonderful mercy and grace. Of course, the price for Him to do that was infinitely steep. It required Jesus as the sacrifice and payment for our sins. But God, who is rich in mercy, was willing to bear that cost. The fusion of truth and mercy is a truly amazing core of the Gospel of Christ.

In our little Plymouth Brethren church in Portland, we used to sing without accompaniment at the Lord's Supper every Sunday. This was one of my favorite hymns. (It was sung to the tune, "God save the queen"). Note the second verse. And you might try singing it to Him.

1 GLORY to God on high, Peace upon earth and joy, Goodwill to man! We who God's blessing prove, His name all names above, Sing now the Saviour's love, Too vast to scan.
2 Mercy and truth unite, Oh, 'tis a wondrous sight, All sights above! Jesus the curse sustains, Guilt's bitter cup He drains, Nothing for us remains, Nothing but love.

3 Love that no tongue can teach, Love that no thought can reach, No love like His! God is its blessed source, Death ne'er can stop its course, Nothing can stay its force, Matchless it is.
4 Blest in this love we sing, To God our praises bring, All sins forgiven: Jesus, our Lord, to Thee Honor and majesty Now and forever be Here, and in heaven. Amen and amen.

(Thomas Kelly, 1769-1854)

Exodus 15:11

"Who is like You, O LORD, among the gods? Who is like You,
glorious in holiness, Fearful in praises, doing wonders?"

As I read this praise song sung by the Israelites to Yahweh as they witnessed their enemies destroyed in the Red Sea before their eyes, it brought to mind worship in our day. Their first expression of worship is the absolute uniqueness of God. To begin in any other way is possibly not worship at all! Israel had seen an unbelievable, awe-inspiring deliverance. Something God alone could do. What has God done in my life that He alone can accomplish? That is the take off point for worship.

"Glorious in holiness". One of God's characteristics that make Him unique and inspires our worship is His holiness. He is uniquely uncommon. He is special, special, special .. the words of Isaiah when he heard the angelic host giving their praise to God. "Holy, holy, holy is the Lord God Almighty."

We need our times of absolute wonder on the far side of the Red Sea to re-establish the wonders of our God, His awesome Presence, His entirely unique specialness. There is nobody and nothing that can equal Him.

Proverbs 10:19, 13:3

"When words are many, transgression is not lacking, but whoever restrains his lips is prudent."
"Whoever guards his mouth preserves his life; he who opens wide his lips comes to ruin."

These two proverbs of Solomon struck me this morning. They offer a quantitative evaluation of the words of the wise versus the foolish person. Interesting that by simply counting my daily word usage will help me evaluate my level of wisdom. Solomon always counsels to speak sparingly and carefully so that I avoid blurting out nonsense.

Often, we want to verbalize our thoughts. Solomon counsels against that. Once a thought is articulated, it enters the world of human interaction. It is subject to interpretation and misunderstanding. Wouldn't it be better to let the thought simmer in our minds a little longer before speaking it? And we might find it isn't necessary speech at all.

James has another way of saying this; *"quick to listen, slow to speak, slow to anger."* James 1:19

Proverbs 1:4-5

4 .. for teaching shrewdness to the inexperienced, knowledge and discretion to a young man —
5 let a wise person listen and increase learning, and let a discerning person obtain guidance.

In other words, the Proverbs are for fathers, sons/daughters and grandfathers. Let's make sure Tahlon, Ben, Declan, Asa, Rilynn (and soon that sixth grandchild) are raised on a steady diet of these wonderful truths. Let's keep the book of Proverbs in front of them constantly.

Ezekiel 18:31-32

31 "Throw off all the transgressions you have committed, and get yourselves
a new heart and a new spirit. Why should you die, house of Israel?
32 "For I take no pleasure in anyone's death." This is the
declaration of the Lord GOD. "So repent and live!

No need for much comment in these verses from the prophet in exile, Ezekiel. He had been taken into captivity from where he continued to tell his people how they might yet please God. The message: repent. We aren't in exile yet, but these words certainly apply to Christians in America too.

Genesis 2:1

"So the heavens and the earth and everything in them were completed."

I have read that verse dozens of times. But as often happens in reading God's Word, a new thought came to me this morning. The text say God's creative work in the cosmos was completed. Finished. Notice it doesn't say evolving. Yet to be determined. It is a fait accompli.

That brings further gravity to the final words of Jesus on the cross, "It is finished." Nothing further to add to the atoning work of Christ for sin. The question for both the creative and redemptive work of God is this: "Do I believe it?"

Revelation 17:14

"These will make war against the Lamb, but the Lamb will conquer them because he is Lord of lords and King of kings. Those with him are called, chosen, and faithful."

Here is a wonderful verse that amplifies a couple points our Reformed brethren make about the believer. Notice that Christians here are labeled as chosen, a cardinal principle of reformed thought. But right behind that is the second principle, faithful. What a privilege to be chosen of God. And what a duty to be faithful to that calling. May He find us faithful in our love and obedience to Christ.

Acts 20:24

A brief word of encouragement from the Apostle Paul in his missionary endeavors this morning.

"But I consider my life of no value to myself; my purpose is to finish my course and the ministry I received from the Lord Jesus, to testify to the gospel of God's grace."

Being a finisher is a great challenge. How easy to start something but get distracted, weary, disinterested along the way. I think of how Brooke courageously set her focus on that finish line at the Charleston Marathon, 26.2 miles away. The distance seemed super human to me. But she had trained for the task. And by increments in her preparation, she worked herself to the point that a finish was possible. And then, she did it!

What an appropriate analogy for the Christian life. The incremental acts of obedience to our Lord condition us for further works of service, enabling us to complete the race He has marked out for each of us.

Have a good run today!

Deuteronomy 30:2

I was struck by the expectation of faith and obedience God asks, even commands from His people in this verse.

> *"and you and your children return to the LORD your God and obey him with all your heart and all your soul by doing everything I am commanding you today."*

Faith in Christ is not a partial past-time. It is not a casual exercise or conscience clean-up from a spasm of guilt. It's not religion that I practice on a few weekends a month or year.

Faith is a worldview. It is a life-consuming exercise of becoming the person God wants me to be. It is the shaper of my thoughts, my beliefs and my desires.

"May it be more like that every day in my life, O Lord my God."

Ruth 1:20-21

> *20 "Don't call me Naomi. Call me Mara," she answered, "for the Almighty has made me very bitter. 21 "I went away full, but the LORD has brought me back empty."*

It is a new year for our family. And what a contrast we have looking forward compared to this poor woman of the Old Testament, Naomi.

Her comment to neighbors upon her return from the land of Moab struck me this morning. She and her family were forced from their homes by a severe famine in the land. There was literally nothing to eat.

So much of human history is the story of how people have struggled to avoid starvation. Isn't it wonderful how our modern agricultural methods have virtually ended that cycle in our lives. Agronomy, irrigation, fertilization and transportation have removed from three generations the threat of starvation in America.

But Naomi and her family lived in a different, less abundant corner of history. So they set out in the all-too-common exodus for food. It is that condition she calls "full" in the verse. "I went away full."

In what sense, Naomi, was your life full? You, your husband and two sons were starving. But the fullness she speaks of referred to her family. Yes, they lacked food, the most basic stuff of life. But they had each other. Their temporal situation, though dire, paled in comparison.

As we look forward to this New Year, isn't our greatest resource and gift each other? What do I need that I don't have if I have all of you in my life. Truly I can say with Naomi "my life is full."

Haggai 2:18

"From this day on, think carefully; from the twenty-fourth day of the ninth month, from the day the foundation of the LORD's temple was laid; think carefully."

I like the instruction God gives His people in this verse. They are returning from 70 years of exile in Babylon for having disobeyed the law of God. A second chance had been given them. God says don't blow it. Don't presume on my grace. Consider carefully your choices, your plans, your desires. Think. And pray.

This verse endorses what is lacking in our modern world, a reflective life. We crowd our minds with the banal .. websites, facebook. That leaves little room for reflection on God, His Word, our circumstances, thoughts and attitudes. Think carefully, Scripture enjoins us. Let's leave some room for that.

Revelation 5:9-10

Here is a glimpse of what the future holds for the Christian.

> 9 *"And they sang a new song, saying: "You (that is Jesus Christ) are worthy to take the scroll, And to open its seals; For You were slain, And have redeemed us to God by Your blood Out of every tribe and tongue and people and nation, 10 And have made us kings and priests to our God; And we shall reign on the earth."*

When Christ returns for the 1000 year earthly reign, guess who comes with Him to administer His righteousness? The Church. Good time now to carefully study the Word to be prepared for that awesome future assignment!

Tahlon: the millennial governor of NC? Declan: Secretary of State? Rilynn: President?

Jason and family, 2019

2 Chronicles 34:27-28

27 *"Because your heart was tender and you humbled yourself before God when you heard his words against this place and against its inhabitants, and because you humbled yourself before me, and you tore your clothes and wept before me, I myself have heard' — this is the LORD's declaration.*
28 *"'I will indeed gather you to your fathers, and you will be gathered to your grave in peace. Your eyes will not see all the disaster that I am bringing on this place and on its inhabitants'"*

Here is the value of real, heart-felt repentance. It saved the life and reign of Israel's last good king Josiah and forestalled God's judgment on the nation. Never too late to change. Never too bad to cry out for divine mercy. Never a hopeless situation when repentance is on the horizon.

A good reminder for our daily lives given then Israelites so many thousands of years ago. It remains just as true and relevant today.

Deut. 13:4 *"You must follow the LORD your God and fear him. You must keep his commands and listen to him; you must worship him and remain faithful to him.*

Praying for all of you today that God will direct your paths as you trust in Him.

Nahum 1:9

The prophet Nahum is an interesting book of the Old Testament. It is the other half of Jonah. If you remember, Jonah went to Nineveh to prophesy destruction unless that nation repented. And Nineveh did repent and forestalled divine judgement.

But 150 years have passed and Nineveh has fallen back into depravity. Nahum prophesied its destruction and this time it was totally destroyed. (It's ruins are in Iraq to this day). This verse caught my eye:

"Whatever you plot against the LORD, he will bring it to complete destruction; oppression will not rise up a second time."

This is a reaping and sowing axiom we find throughout Scripture, made specific to final judgment. The very thing evil people or nations plot against God He will turn against them as their ultimate punishment.

Imagine the voices of the unborn crying out against America's leaders who defend and even support abortion. A day of reckoning is coming for all such unrighteousness, just as it came for Nineveh.

2 Chronicles 21:20

"Jehoram was thirty-two years old when he became king; he reigned eight years in Jerusalem. He died to no one's regret and was buried in the city of David but not in the tombs of the kings."

Read King Jehoram's sorry story in the 21st chapter. This evil king in Judah was the grandson of Asa, a great and godly ruler and the son of Jehoshaphat, who exceeded his father Asa as an excellent king. What a contrast! In a single generation the positive heritage can be overturned.

I was also thinking about Billy Graham's funeral this Friday and that he is being honored in the nation's Capitol for the next two days. How will we be remembered by others when our final day is past? Will it be like Dr. Graham who is given honor and respect or like this man Jehoram who nobody missed? It's a good question to ask myself and to set a course that will result in honor rather than infamy.

Acts 9:31

"So the church throughout all Judea, Galilee, and Samaria had peace and was strengthened. Living in the fear of the Lord and encouraged by the Holy Spirit, it increased in numbers."

Here are four excellent markers to meditate on in the Christian life. Being at peace with God and with each other. Living in peace strengthens us, relationally, emotionally and spiritually.

Maintaining a relationship with the Father through a deep, deep respect - fear of the Lord.

Then there is the encouragement that comes from the Holy Spirit. Nothing is beyond His ability in my life. "I can do all things through Christ who gives me the strength ".

And finally, increase. God prospering my life and in every way imaginable.

Will we live this way? I pray so!!

1 John 3: 1

"See what great love the Father has given us that we should be called God's children — and we are!"

What a wonderful God! Not only has he created us, given us new life in Christ, but He also loves us. Blessed God. What can I give to You this day but my praise and worship?

In Perth, Australia this morning rejoicing in God.

2 Peter 1:2

A word from the Word for my loved ones as I sit in Adelaide, Australia this Saturday morning.

"May grace and peace be multiplied to you through the knowledge of God and of Jesus our Lord."

Here is an important reason to seek a closer, deeper knowledge of the Savior .. it yields more grace and more peace in our lives. That especially relates to sin which easily entangles our lives. By living close to Christ we can experience the joy of a righteous, daily life.

May He re-produce that Christ-like character in each of us this day.

Psalm 139:2-3, 7-10

Here is a blessed truth about God's knowledge and presence in our lives, and one I am acutely aware of being 11 time zones away in Perth, Australia.

2 You know me when I sit down and when I stand up; you understand my thoughts from far away.

3 You observe my travels and my rest; you are aware of all my ways.

7 Where can I go to escape your Spirit? Where can I flee from your presence?

8 If I go up to heaven, you are there; if I make my bed in Sheol, you are there.

9 If I live at the eastern horizon or settle at the western limits,

10 even there your hand will lead me; your right hand will hold on to me.

A political/cultural observation, if you will permit me. What the Psalmist writes about the divine presence in our lives could also be said of Google! The reach of the internet is global and ubiquitous. We virtually cannot escape virtual reality. Which, to me, is a rather unsettling thought. Better to let the Word of God shape our thoughts than the content of the internet, be it Facebook, Twitter, etc.

Psalm 117: 1-2

1 Praise the LORD, all nations! Glorify him, all peoples!
2 For his faithful love to us is great; the LORD's faithfulness endures forever. Hallelujah!

Those two verses are the entire Psalm 117, the shortest psalm of all 150 written in our Bibles. I did some research on it. Of the 1189 chapters in the entire bible, this is the 595th, the exact midpoint of Gods revelation to mankind for the ages. It is the fulcrum point of what God wants to reveal about Himself. And in these two short verses God reveals some precious truth.

God wants us to know He is faithful. We can count on him. When everything else seems to be coming apart, he hinges it all back together. He is our fulcrum on which all things turn. And Gods faithfulness is expressed in the greatest of all concepts He has given to us, His love. In fact, faithfulness is at the very heart of love. God's love is not episodic. It is not performance based. It is faithful. It endures despite our unfaithfulness. It never waivers. It always seeks our best and guides us into truth.

Few words can have such impact as this 117th psalm. Here they reassure us, in the very heart and core of Scripture, that GOD IS LOVE. Hallelujah!

1 Kings 2:2

"As for me, I am going the way of all of the earth. Be strong and be a man."

How often a simple statement in Scripture is loaded with a truth that brings clarity to life. This statement by King David on his deathbed spoken to his heir Solomon is one such example. David calls his immanent death "The way of all the earth." That set me to thinking about birth, life and death - the cycle that all living things experience.

We have recently attended the funerals of two much-loved relatives. They completed their life journeys, this "way of all the earth." It is a time of reflection, mourning, comfort, and ultimately gratitude. Life is precious. What we experience and ultimately leave behind for others to remember and experience vicariously is a central part of life's meaning.

As I attended these memorials I reflected on my life, what is past, what may yet come. Three quarters of my lifespan is behind me now. Most of it. But a significant part remains. How will I use that? How will you?

David's advice to Solomon gives some good direction. First, be strong. Life cycles are part of every living thing on earth - "the way of all the earth". Some insects have life spans of only days. Mice have the shortest spans of mammals. There are whales with life spans of two centuries. Some trees live for thousands of years.

I will be fortunate to see 90 years. So be strong in those allotted years, David says. Get the most from them. Don't waste them through fear or idleness or ignorance.

And be a man. I would say to Rilynn, "be the woman God intends you to be." Be fully everything you possibly can. Leave nothing undone. Maximize your God-given gifts and talents. This is your stage. This is your opportunity to experience this amazing thing called human life. Get all you can from it.

As I review the seven decades of my life, there is great satisfaction. But there remains much to be done. I want to grow in godliness in my remaining years. I want to be more like Jesus. I also want to build on the legacy I was given by my ancestors. I want to leave something behind for my children and grandchildren that they will value.

This is the "way of all the earth ". And it is an engaging path. I am so very thankful to be on it.

Daniel 9:13

"Just as it is written in the law of Moses, all this disaster has come on us, yet we have not sought the favor of the LORD our God by turning from our iniquities and paying attention to your truth."

Daniel wrote this from exile. He and the nation of Israel had been driven from their land decades before because they refused to repent of sin. Isn't it interesting how hard the human heart can become in its refusal to turn back to God. Despite all they endured, yet they would not turn back to their God.

And this hardness seems to multiply in our lives. What we would hardly do before can become a regular practice if it continues in our lives. This hardening of our consciences toward wrong-doing is one of the consequences of unconfessed sin.

"O beloved, may we remain softened to the voice of the Lord. And when He speaks into our lives be quick to respond."

John 1:10-12

Here is a wonderful passage for consideration this morning:

10 He was in the world, and the world was created through him, and yet the world did not recognize him.
11 He came to his own, and his own people did not receive him.
12 But to all who did receive him, he gave them the right to be
children of God, to those who believe in his name.

Look at the problem of verses 10 and 11. When Jesus came people did not recognize him (v 10) or receive him (v 11). Recognizing Jesus for who he is so critical. He is the Son of God. He is the Word made flesh. He is the light of the world. He is the Savior.

Recognizing precedes receiving. That allows me to fully enter into a relationship with Him by receiving Him as He is (described in verse 12). It is so important to teach our children who Jesus is, the only begotten Son of God! And that by receiving Him through faith we can be God's children.

And there is no other way of salvation than that!

Psalm 78:1-7

1 My people, hear my instruction; listen to the words from my mouth.

2 I will declare wise sayings; I will speak mysteries from the past —

3 things we have heard and known and that our fathers have passed down to us.

4 We will not hide them from their children, but will tell a future generation the praiseworthy

acts of the LORD, his might, and the wondrous works he has performed.

5 He established a testimony in Jacob and set up a law in Israel, which

he commanded our fathers to teach to their children

6 so that a future generation —children yet to be born — might

know. They were to rise and tell their children

7 so that they might put their confidence in God and not forget God's works, but keep his commands.

An O'Connell family member used this text for a devotional at the family reunion/celebration today. He focused on the responsibility of one generation to the next by planting the truth of God in the hearts of our children and grandchildren. Our patriarch and his wife were strongly affirmed as our family example of this. They have prayed for the salvation of their family and even helped many of us with Christian Marriage Encounter weekends they paid for.

Then a remarkable moment to close the hour long study. One of the grandchildren shared how he has been free of alcohol for 16 months after it had begun destroying his life.

For a quiet, introverted young man, it was a powerful and poignant moment that brought great joy to the entire family. What a privilege to belong to a family of faith where God is at work to redeem and rebuild our lives. To Him belongs the praise and honor.

2 Samuel 7:29

"Now, please bless your servant's house so that it will continue before you forever. For you, Lord GOD, have spoken, and with your blessing your servant's house will be blessed forever."

As David prayed for his family in this great prayer of dedication, so today is a day of prayer for our house.

"Lord Jesus, please send peace and security on Jason and Stacey's family. Bless the work of their hands and give them favor with every contact they make. Grant them wisdom and grace as they raise Tahlon, Declan and Rilynn. Grant Tahlon increased capacity to learn and give him gifts from above to serve You. Open Declan and Rilynn's hearts early to the gospel of Your grace. Guard them physically from sickness or injury. Reveal Your Son to them at an early age that they may believe and receive Him as Savior. "Watch over John as he serves in a distant land. Open the door of opportunity for him to serve in ways that You have enabled him. Guide John in a path of righteousness for Your name sake. Bring joy and contentment to his path this day.

"Bless the home of Jared and Brooke. Strengthen them in their love for You and for each other. Grant them wisdom in their instructions to Ben and Asa. Protect the boys from illness and error and bring them the faith to believe in Jesus as their Savior. Guard this new life You have graciously given them. And bring him into their family with great joy.

"And I thank You Lord for each member of this family. In Jesus Name .."

Christmas, 2019

2 Timothy 1:9

"He has saved us and called us with a holy calling, not according to our works, but according to his own purpose and grace, which was given to us in Christ Jesus before time began."

At times like these, the passing of a dearly loved friend/relative, this verse brings comfort and clarity. Upon reflection, the journey of faith now completed by our brother-in-law is so clearly outlined in this verse.

Stage 1 - salvation. "..he saved us..". I was with Scott in the Summer of 1981 when he bowed his head and heart to God and trusted Christ as his Savior.

Stage 2 - a holy calling. "..and called us.." God called Scott back to an earlier vow he made as a husband and father. That had slipped a little by that Summer, 1981. But he finished very well on both counts.

Stage 3 – God's purpose. "..to his own purpose.." For every believer His purpose is to glorify His Son. Which we do through good works. Reading Facebook comments leaves the strongest impression about a trail of goodness and mercy that Scott has left behind.

Stage 4 - His grace. This is vital to accomplish stages 1-3. Salvation, calling, purpose all need divine grace to carry out. Scott received the grace he needed and finished the course set out by God. We grieve his loss. But not like those without Christ. Praise our Savior!

Leviticus 16:29

"This is to be a permanent statute for you: In the seventh month, on the tenth day of the month you are to practice self-denial and do no work, both the native and the alien who resides among you."

Leviticus can be an experience! Reading through the various offerings, the sacrificial procedures can seem like a religious anachronism. With the new covenant and the once-for-all sacrifice of Jesus, this all changed. What is the relevance now? Yet there are principles here that can help guide us in the present age, the age of grace. And one of them is the practice of self-denial.

Ours is a historic period of unrivaled abundance. We live in times of unparalleled access to food, housing, clothing .. not only the basic necessities but a myriad of other luxury things. Travel, entertainment, leisure, saving, the list goes on and on. At no time in human history has the common person enjoyed the fruits of prosperity as now. And through easy credit we are able to seemingly increase our access to this cornucopia of modern convenience and luxury.

I'm not being critical of this abundance. I have fully embraced it. I have two vehicles, two houses, two bank accounts, two sets of tools. You get my gist. So the idea of self-denial can seem terribly foreign, even antiquated. With the daily barrage of marketing that tells me I deserve more (!) how can this idea of limiting my access by choice be relevant? But it is important now, perhaps more than ever. Because the Bible warns that this excess easily becomes a type of idolatry replacing my dependence and gratitude toward the Giver.

And idolatry is the first and gravest offense in the Ten Commandments - "you shall have no other gods before you." So fasting is a helpful antidote to a mindless participation in our present abundance: Taking a break from the "plenty" for prayer, for self-examination, for new or renewed focus on other things. The simple act of self- denial is one way of reviewing where I stand with everything around me and to make sure nothing has replaced my love and dependence on Him.

Lamentations 5:21

"LORD, bring us back to yourself, so we may return; renew our days as in former times."

I really like this verse. It captures the cry we offer up to God when a particular attitude or action has snared us for the umpteenth time. It gives the instruction and action we can take to draw near to God when sin and unrighteousness has made us feel distant. That is the nature of sin. It causes us to fall short of His glory. It is the path to death and separation from Him. But what good news to remember that God beckons us to return. *"Lord bring us back to Yourself!"*

How easy it seems to wander away either intentionally or out of neglect. Whichever, we suddenly find ourselves distant and removed from the Lord.

When I was a boy, our family would sometimes go for walks to the park. I remember playing a silly game; lingering behind, watching the distance between myself and my parents grow. I would let it get just so far before they would stop and call on me to hurry up .. or before they did that, I would decide the distance was too great and run to catch up. It was my little game to see how much distance I could stand before returning to their side. Being near my parents was security. It was safe. It was comfortable. We often play the same game with God. "Let me see how far I can stray before He draws me back or I get too uncomfortable being away." Strange game when I was a kid. Even stranger now that I am an adult. Jesus wants me next to Him.

It is safe and secure and peaceful close to Him. *"Come to me all who are weary and heavy burdened"*. Matthew 11:28. His offer is constant. He is waiting if you are living at a distance.

Exodus 1:22

So Pharaoh commanded all his people, saying, "Every son who is born you
shall cast into the river, and every daughter you shall save alive."

Consider the consequences of a society that practiced infanticide and abortion as a public policy. In Egypt, during the era of Moses, such a policy was used to control the Israelite people. In fact, Moses should have been a victim of that official policy as were thousands of other Hebrew children. But God had other purposes for this child. As an offspring of the Egyptian culture of death, it was easy for Moses to take another's life. In the next chapter we read of Moses taking the life of an Egyptian who was mistreating an Israelite. Life loses its sacredness in a culture of death. It is easily tossed aside.

And what about America where nearly one million abortions will take the lives of children this year? And in some states live births can now legally be ended if chosen by the mother. How can this end well for America? If there is a Judge in Heaven, we will have to give an account for these barbaric practices. Take a moment today and celebrate the lives of this new generation of Matthews children. They are great gifts. They are cherished. They are irreplaceable. They are our greatest assets, our finest rewards. We love them dearly. We defend them completely. They ARE the culture of life we build for the future.

Psalm 90: 10, 12

10 Our lives last seventy years or, if we are strong, eighty years. Even the best of
them are struggle and sorrow; indeed, they pass quickly and we fly away.
12 Teach us to number our days carefully so that we may develop wisdom in our hearts.

As my 70th year approaches, been thinking about all that is past and anticipating what is yet to come. God has been so good to me. So were my parents, my siblings, my wife, my children. I have lived a most pleasant existence. But the numbers don't lie. Most of my life is in the rear view mirror. It is sweet to think back on the wealth of experiences I have had with all of you. They are my most cherished possession. If my longevity is similar to my parents (and I hope it is!), more than 3/4s of life is finished. That leaves me 20 more years. How will those final years be spent? What sorts of memories can still be built? What kinds of opportunities to serve Christ await me? The first third of my life I lived for my own selfish desires. Then Christ showed me the more excellent way, serving Him and others. Like Paul, I want to finish the race well. I want to run the course God laid out for me. How about you? Some of you are only a third into this race. There's much more left. Others half way through. Still others getting toward the final third or even quarter of the race. Will we run well for Him? Will the memories be sweet and will we leave behind an example for our offspring to follow?

1 Corinthians 3:2-3

2 I gave you milk to drink, not solid food, since you were not yet ready for it. In fact, you are still not ready, 3 because you are still worldly. For since there is envy and strife among you, are you not worldly and behaving like mere humans.

I was thinking about Asa and Rilynn when I read these verses this morning. Asa is a little ahead of Rilynn in eating solid food. Isn't it interesting how our bodies adjust from that initial nourishment of mama's milk to the food all around us? The spiritual truth this illustrates is Paul's challenge to the Corinthians. He is telling them to grow up and start getting spiritual nourishment in an adult way. They were spiritual babies too long. They had stayed at the Rilynn level and had not progressed to Asa and beyond.

Teeth are the biggest physical development that lets Asa eat solid food. In the spiritual world, it is not the lack of something (teeth) that Paul indicates as immature, but the fact there is still envy and strife in the lives of the spiritually immature. A growing Christian removes those things and replaces them with thanksgiving and peace. Every time I look at Asa I am reminded to be thankful and at peace with others. That is the "feast" of the Christian life.

1 Corinthians 4:9-13

9 For I think God has displayed us, the apostles, in last place like men condemned to die:
We have become a spectacle to the world, both to angels and to people.
10 We are fools for Christ, but you are wise in Christ! We are weak, but
you are strong! You are distinguished, but we are dishonored!
11 Up to the present hour we are both hungry and thirsty; we
are poorly clothed, roughly treated, homeless;
12 we labor, working with our own hands. When we are reviled,
we bless; when we are persecuted, we endure it;
13 when we are slandered, we respond graciously. Even now, we are
like the scum of the earth, like everyone's garbage.

As I read through those verses I found myself thinking, "I sure wouldn't want to be one of the 12 apostles." That is a difficult calling, and one I surely don't want! Of course, Paul had to write the 16th verse.

16 Therefore I urge you to imitate me.

Gulp! That will need much grace to attempt or even contemplate. What more can I say…

Matthew 9:2

Just then some men brought to him a paralytic lying on a stretcher. Seeing their
faith, Jesus told the paralytic, "Have courage, son, your sins are forgiven."

Isn't it interesting how Jesus addresses this need. Here is an obvious physical need brought to him. And only he can meet that need .. a paralytic. But Jesus first deals with a deeper, more crucial need in this man's life .. a spiritual and eternal one. The man's problem was sin. Same with me.

I want God to solve a physical/temporal issue in my life. But He focuses on the unseen/permanent. And only Christ can handle that greater problem of sin in my life.

> 6 *"But so that you may know that the Son of Man has authority on earth to forgive*
> *sins" — then he told the paralytic, "Get up, take your stretcher, and go home."*

What a wonderful Savior! He didn't let the man leave with His physical defect. But neither did He prioritize it. James says in his NT letter "every good and perfect gift is from above", a truth perfectly illustrated by the Lord Jesus in this passage.

Read the whole account in Matthew 9:1-7 for a greater blessing.

Romans 1:12

".. that is, to be mutually encouraged by each other's faith, both yours and mine."

Here is a key component of a Christian family. It is simple, too. We need to be encouraging each others' faith. This family encourages well. We encourage our love of Duck football. (BEAT THE DAWGS TODAY!!). We affirm and encourage each family member when they celebrate birthdays. We help and encourage when we have problems, projects (backyard decks, tree houses) and opportunities.

Encouraging our faith in Jesus Christ is another of those key areas of encouragement we must attend to. That encouragement makes it possible that none of us will fall away from the faith; that the little ones will grow up in the faith; that still unsaved family members will change direction and give their lives to Christ in faith. Being mutually encouraged in faith is so important to the spiritual well-being of our family.

Let's find ways to actively encourage our faith in the coming season of thanksgiving and Christmas, two of the most faith-centered celebrations we have. Let's stir each other to love and good deeds, like serving at the food center. Let's challenge each other to remain faithful in weekly worship with other believers and giving to the needs of others. Let's be mutual encouragers.

Psalm 101:1-6

This psalm is a song to integrity, being undivided. In English, the root word comes from the term integer, a whole number in math. It is mentioned three times in these few verses.

1 I will sing of faithful love and justice; I will sing praise to you, LORD.
*2 I will pay attention to the way of **integrity**. When will you come to*
*me? I will live with a heart of **integrity** in my house.*
3 I will not let anything worthless guide me. I hate the practice of transgression; it will not cling to me.
4 A devious heart will be far from me; I will not be involved with evil.
5 I will destroy anyone who secretly slanders his neighbor; I cannot
tolerate anyone with haughty eyes or an arrogant heart.
6 My eyes favor the faithful of the land so that they may sit down with
*me. The one who follows the way of **integrity** may serve me.*

That third verse jumped out at me this morning. Sin has a way of clinging to us dividing us from the true path. It is a perverse relationship of attraction .. it attracts us, we are attracted to it. It clings when not dealt with through confession and repentance. "Lord, deliver me from the power of sin's grip so it cannot cling to me!"

1 Corinthians 6:9-11

9 Do you not know that the unrighteous will not inherit the kingdom of God? Do not be deceived.
Neither fornicators, nor idolaters, nor adulterers, nor homosexuals, nor sodomites,
10 nor thieves, nor covetous, nor drunkards, nor revilers, nor extortioners will inherit the kingdom of God.
11 And such were some of you. But you were washed, but you were sanctified, but you
were justified in the name of the Lord Jesus and by the Spirit of our God.

Here is the message the Apostle Paul would have for our culture and the LGBTQ movement. There is no connection between these behaviors and what God is doing in His redemptive work among us. And the same sex behaviors are not more or less offensive than heterosexual sin like sex before marriage (fornication) or adultery (sex outside marriage). But acceptance of any of those behaviors is denial of God's law.

And there is only one remedy for those caught up in them, whether hereto- or homosexual. It is the good news of that 11th verse. Be washed in the blood of Christ. Be set apart for holy things. Be declared justified before the Righteous Judge by faith in His Son.

I am so thankful my father found God's way out of his sexual perversion. One of the greatest moments of my life was a call I received from him on a Saturday morning following a deep conversation we had the night before about the Gospel. I shared with him my testimony and how I had put my faith in Jesus Christ as my savior. I challenged my dad to consider this pathway for his life.

And that's exactly what he did. He called me that Saturday morning and said these exact words "a miracle took place last night, son. I accepted Christ as my savior! I'm now a follower of Jesus." His life changed. And I am eternally thankful for the washing, the sanctifying work of the Spirit and God's justification that took place when he yielded to Jesus Christ. It remains one of the most remarkable events I look back upon.

Jeremiah 30:19

As we approach the Thanksgiving season, I found a wonderful verse that could serve as a spiritual foundation for the celebration.

19 Then out of them shall proceed thanksgiving and the voice of those who make merry; I will multiply them, and they shall not diminish; I will also glorify them, and they shall not be small.

With the additions of Declan, Asa and Rilynn we can certainly see this promise fulfilled in our family. What a cause for thanksgiving!

Isaiah 53: 1-6

On this Thanksgiving Day (2019) I could list a thousand reasons to be thankful - children, grandchildren, health, abundant provision, good work; the list goes on and on. Maybe we can share some of those things today at dinner. And Isaiah reminds me of the greatest blessing and one to be most thankful for.

1 Who has believed what we have heard? And to whom has the arm of the LORD been revealed? 2 He grew up before him like a young plant and like a root out of dry ground. He didn't have an impressive form or majesty that we should look at him, no appearance that we should desire him. 3 He was despised and rejected by men, a man of suffering who knew what sickness was. He was like someone people turned away from; he was despised, and we didn't value him. 4 Yet he himself bore our sicknesses, and he carried our pains; but we in turn regarded him stricken, struck down by God, and afflicted. 5 But he was pierced because of our rebellion, crushed because of our iniquities; punishment for our peace was on him, and we are healed by his wounds. 6 We all went astray like sheep; we all have turned to our own way; and the LORD has punished him for the iniquity of us all.

Luke 11:13

"If you then, being evil, know how to give good gifts to your children, how much more will your heavenly Father give the Holy Spirit to those who ask Him!"

What is more attractive than a one year old learning new things. Life is unfolding for Rilynn. Delightful. We get to shower her with gifts this weekend, her first birthday. We will be illustrating Jesus' teaching. But that little comment He made about "you being evil" is just a little off-putting. Jesus was a truth-teller, regardless of the audience. He spoke plain truth to his disciples, his friends, his enemies .. even his mother. And the truth is this; we are all born with a hereditary disease called sin.

Even in that precious little girl, Rilynn, sin lurks waiting to make itself known. As my father used to say "she's still a member of the holiness club" (she is not yet accountable for her sin, but that day is coming soon). The rest of us need salvation and right now! That is what makes Jesus offer so valuable. He is saying if we ask God, He will give us a holy Presence to battle the evil of our souls. That gift is a member of the Triune Godhead, the Holy Spirit to fill me with His power and provide the control I need to overcome sin. What wonderful gifts God is willing to give just for the asking.

Will you ask him today?

Revelation 1:12-15

12 Then I turned to see whose voice it was that spoke to me.
When I turned I saw seven golden lampstands,
13 and among the lampstands was one like the Son of Man, dressed in
a robe and with a golden sash wrapped around his chest.
14 The hair of his head was white as wool — white as snow — and his eyes like a fiery flame.
15 His feet were like fine bronze as it is fired in a furnace, and his voice like the sound of cascading waters.

Peter says in his first letter, *"though you have not seen Him (Christ), you love Him."* 1 Peter 1:8. Can you imagine what it will be like seeing Jesus Christ in glory for the first time? John gives the picture of what He is like on the throne of heaven. It is awesome, almost beyond words.

I focused this morning on his voice. Recently Gwen, Tahlon and I hiked to Soco Falls on the road to Cherokee. It had rained hard the previous week and the waters were rushing off the mountain. The sound of that rushing water was mesmerizing. It was also comforting. We sat there listening, watching the water splash off the rocks as it cascaded down the slope. It was a thousand voices with varying pitches.

I can't imagine what it will be like to actually hear Jesus speak to me in heaven. But that experience at the falls and these words of John give me something to expect. Jesus' voice will be comforting. It will be pervasive. It will be infinitely varied so as to reach every personality hearing Him. It will be front and center, yet filling the background simultaneously. Just like Soco Falls.

Soco Falls, near Maggie Valley, NC, 2019

John 12:44-45

44 Jesus cried out, "The one who believes in me believes not in me, but in him who sent me.
45 "And the one who sees me sees him who sent me.

If I could define myself in a single word it would be "explorer". For my entire life I have been intrigued and captured by the discovery of new places, new ideas. This started at a very young age when our family would go to different destinations around the Northwest .. beach towns, mountain retreats, Montana and Idaho destinations. I always loved seeing, hearing, smelling these various places. The "way" forward was always the backseat of our family car. I would occupy one side; my sister the other. At the outset there was anticipation and good feelings. We often sang hymns and other popular songs as a family. Inevitably, boredom with hours of driving (particularly driving to Montana) set in and fights erupted in the backseat. Our parents would find ways to distract us by playing games .. the ABC game on road signs, the "guess who I am" game and others like it. As we neared the destination anticipation grew over seeing and experiencing another new place.

How I loved to travel and explore. Jesus had a mission when He came to earth from heaven .. bring people back to the Father. He made it clear there was only one route to heaven and eternal life:

Himself. *"I am the way, the truth and the life."* John 14:6. Spiritual travelers can only get to that eternal destination through Christ. There is no other way. If I want to know God, if I want a relationship with the Father it must be through the Son. To believe in, to see and experience the Divine can only be done through Jesus Christ. Not my words. They are His. It is what frustrates modern sensitivities. Too narrow. Too restrictive. But according to Jesus, it is true.

2 Timothy 2:19

"Nevertheless, God's solid foundation stands firm, bearing this inscription: The Lord knows those who are his, and let everyone who calls on the name of the Lord turn away from wickedness."

I have been spending much time considering the value of foundations. In the newest addition to EvenRidge, we spent considerable time planning and building the right foundation. It has been complicated. The ground was sloping and forced the construction of a retaining wall to gain a level surface to build on. That foundation wall required two essential elements: concrete blocks and rebar. The concrete supports the downward pressure of the building. The rebar supports the horizontal pressure of the gravel fill against the brick walls. Without both, the foundation would fail.

It is the same in the Christian life. The Lord is the source of our strength against the pressures of this world. He is the chief cornerstone of our salvation. Without God's work and presence in our lives we would collapse spiritually. God uses our obedience to His Word as the other necessary support. It is what we bring to the strength of our salvation. Turning away from evil is our rebar. Together, we have the firm foundation on which to build the Christian life.

"The Nest" Construction Project, 2019

Hebrews 4:12

For the word of God is living and effective and sharper than any double-edged sword, penetrating as far as the separation of soul and spirit, joints and marrow. It is able to judge the thoughts and intentions of the heart.

A reminder: being a Christian is being a person of the Word of God.

Luke 12:35 *"Be ready for service and have your lamps lit."*

When I read this verse today I thought of our Christmas Day work at Rowan Ministries serving meals. Always ready to serve others. That works for the home too.

Jared, you impressed me when you quickly got up from dinner to clean the kitchen. Our wives had prepared a wonderful meal for the family. You showed gratitude by finishing with the clean-up. Serving. It is the way of Christ.

"For the Son Of Man came not to be served but to serve .." Matthew 20:28.

Psalm 97:11

"Light dawns for the righteous, gladness for the upright in heart."

Here is a combination of truth and joy. Often scripture writers link two concepts and imply their relationship. Here is an example .. when I live in the light (truth, transparency), I can expect the residual benefit of the other (joy, well being).

Psalm 103:2 *Bless the LORD, O my soul, And forget not all His benefits:*
3 Who forgives all your iniquities, Who heals all your diseases,
4 Who redeems your life from destruction, Who crowns you with lovingkindness and tender mercies,
5 Who satisfies your mouth with good things, So that your youth is renewed like the eagle's.

Here is a short list of the benefits of knowing and trusting in Jesus. His gifts to us this and every season: forgiveness, healing, redemption, reward, satisfaction and renewal.

2 Samuel 7:14-15

A good encouragement for the pattern of fatherhood. Here is how God sees Himself as a father.

14 "I will be his father, and he will be my son. When he does wrong, I will discipline him with a rod of men and blows from mortals. 15 "But my faithful love will never leave him as it did when I removed it from Saul, whom I removed from before you.

Discipline and faithful love; the foundations of His parental love. I noticed at EvenRidge this past weekend, that when Declan required a little of his father's discipline, he always heard the words, "I love you" when the discipline was over. That captures the essence of this verse. Disciplining our children is a function of our love for them as it is with our Heavenly Father.

Jason and Declan, 2018

Leviticus 11:45

*"For I am the LORD, who brought you up from the land of Egypt to
be your God, so you must be holy because I am holy."*

God is always the standard by which I evaluate truth, morality, etc. He calls me to enter into that standard through faith and obedience. The one (faith) propels the other (obedience). Can I truly be a person of faith without obedience to His Word?

Proverbs 24:3-4

*3 Through wisdom a house is built, And by understanding it is established;
4 By knowledge the rooms are filled With all precious and pleasant riches.*

As I read these verses this morning, EvenRidge came to mind. The wisdom of our contractor who constructed the building was evident. And the creative knowledge of Gwen to decorate EvenRidge and make it beautiful. What a delight to consider for generations to come: Understanding that can establish EvenRidge. That is the key for all of us. To be wise in our use of it including how we treat each other. Really looking forward to the "establishment" of EvenRidge as a place of rest, inspiration and fellowship.

Mark 6:6

*"And he was amazed at their unbelief.
He was going around the villages teaching."*

The lack of faith limited Jesus' ability to do miraculous works in his hometown of Nazareth. Familiarity with him caused many to reject His divine power. It is the danger of the Christian life too.

We can become so familiar with living under the grace of God that a kind of unbelief sets in. Instead of seeing Gods hand at work in the intimate details of my life, I may ascribe His work to coincidence, luck or good fortune. Better to find the God of every spiritual grace active and involved in giving His limitless gifts of grace.

What a good season to renew that simple faith in the gift-giving God when we give each other gifts at Christmas time.

Christmas, 2017

Judges 6:12

And the Angel of the LORD appeared to him, and said to him,
"The LORD is with you, you mighty man of valor!"

I love this passage and this verse in Judges. Let me set the stage. Israel has fallen away from the Lord. Their enemies have taken back much of the land Joshua had won in the great campaign to establish the nation. The Israelites have fled to the mountains and are living in caves just to survive. The outlook is bleak. Into this crisis steps the angel of the Lord with a visit to Gideon who is also hiding in the mountains eking out an existence. God has great plans for this man, evidenced by the way he addresses Gideon,

"… You mighty man of valor!"

Is it irony? A not-so-subtle dig? A dark joke? Gideon is grinding what little wheat he gathered in a wine vat! It's not a joke! Rather, it is the reality God sees in Gideon. He looks at what can be, not what is. He sees Gideon's potential. God has a vision for Gideon that outweighs his present circumstances.

I like to think it is no different with us. In my struggle to be a Jesus follower with all the character, morality and faith that implies, I am glad that God sees me as I will be, not just as what I am now. He has a vision for my life that far exceeds the limitations of my present reality. Being too caught up in what I am now is a poor way of capturing that vision. That is why faith in Him is at the core of my walk. He will accomplish everything He has set out to do in my life

"Faithful is He who has called you. He will do it."
1 Thessalonians 5:24

Job 19: 25-27

25 But I know that my Redeemer lives, and at the end he will stand on the dust.
26 Even after my skin has been destroyed, yet I will see God in my flesh.
27 I will see him myself; my eyes will look at him, and not as a stranger. My heart longs within me.

This year Christmas has fallen on Wednesday. I could modify my reading schedule to take a passage from Matthew or Luke appropriate to this day. But being a patterned old man (remember I just turned 70), I stick with my reading from the book of Job.

One never expects the joy and mystery of a day like today in Job. It is a treatise on how the righteous deal with grief and loss. And unjust accusations from even their friends. It is not Christmas-type fare. But I am surprised by the passage I encounter, these miracle verses that foretell the greatest gift God has given to mankind. That gift is His Son who was born of the virgin, lived a perfect life, died unjustly and rose again. And who should be the first to realize that in God's good timing the gospel story would all unfold in Bethlehem and Nazareth and finally Golgotha? It was Job.

Here he reveals that God is a Redeemer. His Redeemer. Redemption from the curse of sin is a personal matter. He further grasps that there will be resurrection from the dead. His own resurrection. And he further understands that a personal relationship with this Redeemer God will be his final reward.

Redeemed. Resurrected. Rewarded. Coming from one so buried in trial and grief, that is a real gift on this Christmas. Do you have that same certainty and faith expressed by this great saint of God, Job? It is there for you as a gift of faith if you would receive it from Him.

Revelation 14:12

"This calls for endurance from the saints, who keep God's commands and their faith in Jesus."

I am back to running in the mornings. It is one of those disciplines that requires constant effort. Getting out of bed, putting on those running shoes, stepping out into a still dark world when I would rather be sleeping. It is a matter of self-discipline.

The Christian life is an exercise in discipline too. That is why the Bible refers to believers as disciples. This verse mentions the two key disciplines that mark the Christian. The first is obedience to God's commands. Whether that is responding to His voice speaking into my life (a Holy Spirit guided conscience) or actively seeking His will in daily scripture reading, Christians are people who are led. We obey Him.

The other mentioned here is an active faith in Christ. This faith informs my choices in life. It guides and shapes my relationships with others. It sets my goals and determines my desires. It finishes the course God has marked out for me.

Finishing a run in the morning is harder than starting it. Finishing means overcoming fatigue. I want to quit before the mark is reached. But as in the way of faith, how satisfying and rewarding to reach with the strength I have and make the mark. And in the Christian life, He pushes me on toward the goal .. the upward call of God in Christ Jesus.

Ruth 2:8-9

8 Then Boaz said to Ruth, "Listen, my daughter. Don't go and gather grain in another
field, and don't leave this one, but stay here close to my female servants.
9 "See which field they are harvesting, and follow them. Haven't
I ordered the young men not to touch you?

This good man Boaz is one of my heroes in Scripture. He shows up in the biblical narrative at a time of extreme corruption in Israel when everyone is doing according to their own values and standards instead of following God's Law. But Boaz is not swayed by all the wickedness around him. He persevered in doing what is right.

Increasingly that is what Christians in our age will have to decide: whether to follow the Bible or slip into the way of the culture which is increasingly hostile to biblical values and truth.

And what are the basic values this good man exemplified? He is a protector/provider as shown in these two verses. He took a very vulnerable young woman, Ruth, under his care and protected her from the men around her. And he also provided sustenance for her and her mother-in-law by enabling her to gather grain in his field.

Protector and Provider. It is the pattern God has set for men. It is our basic calling in the family, the church and in society. Our culture fails when men use their strength to intimidate or plunder (example Harvey Weinstein) or to abandon their responsibility to provide.

The biblical pattern is the way of divine order. It enables us to live quiet, peaceful lives as we await a new age to come with Christ in control.

May He find us faithful to the task in that soon-coming Day.

John and Tahlon at the movies

Romans 12:3

"For by the grace given to me, I tell everyone among you not to think of himself more highly than he should think. Instead, think sensibly, as God has distributed a measure of faith to each one."

I appreciate what Paul has brought to my attention this morning. Humility, or thinking not too highly of myself is really a measure of faith. How does that work?

Faith is trusting in an all sufficient God. It is rendering to Him the ultimate role He alone deserves in my life. Assuming His position, being my own master and authority is what faith does not look like. Yielding to Him is putting self and ego on a back burner.

That is the first step for a humble person: acknowledging they aren't the center of their reality. I suppose it is possible for an atheist to be truly humble, but not in this Christian way. Putting God first, others next and myself last is what Jesus calls me to.

That is humility!

Psalm 17:3

"You have tested my heart; you have examined me at night. You have tried me and found nothing evil; I have determined that my mouth will not sin.

How interesting. Night is often accountability time with God. At night our lives slow down. They get quiet. They become reflective so the Spirit can speak.

We are more alone with our thoughts. God has the chance to break through the daily noise. And He does. Conviction, direction, counsel from the Lord often happen at night. It's good to then sleep on the Lord's instructions and re-evaluate in the morning before taking action.

How good to come through these nocturnal sessions with God and say with the Psalmist "You have tried me and found nothing evil." What a delight to live life pleasing to God.

Jeremiah 28:15

*15 The prophet Jeremiah said to the prophet Hananiah, "Listen, Hananiah! The
LORD did not send you, but you have led these people to trust in a lie.
16 "Therefore, this is what the LORD says: 'I am about to send you off the face of the earth.
You will die this year because you have preached rebellion against the LORD.' "
17 And the prophet Hananiah died that year in the seventh month.*

This was a contest between competing visions of God's will for Israel. The false prophet said all was good. No need to worry, repent, change direction.

But God's prophet had the true message - disaster is coming unless there is a change of course. And disaster came when Nebuchadnezzar overran Israel and carted its people off into 70 years of captivity

I thought about the battle ongoing in our day within the Methodist church (and other mainline denominations) where a competing vision of marriage is being fought. The prophetic voice of one side says all is well with same sex unions. In fact, they celebrate them. The other side defends one man-one woman as the only biblical way.

I think we know how this will turn out. The false prophet Hananiah shows us God's judgment on the matter. And it will end in American churches no different than what became of him. In fact, many of these churches are already dying.

Departing from God's Word unleashes a maelstrom of judgment on a nation. My prayer is that we are not beyond redemption. Let's pray today for our leaders in America.

Proverbs 18:22

Read this tonight and gave a hearty amen.

"A man who finds a wife finds a good thing and obtains favor from the LORD."

Go Ducks!

Isaiah 11:1-10

Read and rejoice. What the future holds for this world when Christ returns and reigns.

1 There shall come forth a Rod from the stem of Jesse, And a Branch shall grow out of his roots.
2 The Spirit of the LORD shall rest upon Him, The Spirit of wisdom and understanding,
The Spirit of counsel and might, The Spirit of knowledge and of the fear of the LORD.
3 His delight is in the fear of the LORD, And He shall not judge by the
sight of His eyes, Nor decide by the hearing of His ears;
4 But with righteousness He shall judge the poor, And decide with equity for the meek of the earth; He
shall strike the earth with the rod of His mouth, And with the breath of His lips He shall slay the wicked.
5 Righteousness shall be the belt of His loins, And faithfulness the belt of His waist.
6 "The wolf also shall dwell with the lamb, The leopard shall lie down with the young goat,
The calf and the young lion and the fatling together; And a little child shall lead them.

7 The cow and the bear shall graze; Their young ones shall lie down together; And the lion shall eat straw like the ox.
8 The nursing child shall play by the cobra's hole, And the weaned child shall put his hand in the viper's den.

9 They shall not hurt nor destroy in all my holy mountain, For the earth shall be full of the knowledge of the LORD As the waters cover the sea.
10 "And in that day there shall be a Root of Jesse, Who shall stand as a banner to the people; For the Gentiles shall seek Him, And His resting place shall be glorious."

Amen and amen. Maranatha. Come Lord Jesus.

Printed in the United States
By Bookmasters